Elements of Style
for Preaching

Books in the Craft of Preaching Series

THE CRAFT OF PREACHING SERIES

Elements of Style for Preaching

WILLIAM H. KOOIENGA

Ministry
Resources
Library

Zondervan Publishing House • Grand Rapids, MI

ELEMENTS OF STYLE FOR PREACHING
Copyright © 1989 by William H. Kooienga

Ministry Resources Library is an imprint of Zondervan Publishing House, 1415 Lake Drive, S.E., Grand Rapids, Michigan 49506.

Library of Congress Cataloging in Publication Data

Kooienga, William H.
    Elements of style for preaching / by William H. Kooienga.
       p.   cm. — (Craft of Preaching series)
    Bibliography: p.
    ISBN 0-310-31011-3
    1. Preaching. 2. Rhetoric. 3. English language—Style.
  I. Title. II. Series.
    BV4211.2.K64   1989   88-37111
    808'.066251—dc19

Edited by Joan Johnson and Michael G. Smith
Designed by Louise Bauer

Printed in the United States of America

89 90 91 92 93 94 95 / CH / 10 9 8 7 6 5 4 3 2 1

To Marilyn

Contents

Introduction

 F our church buildings stand near the center of town; they are different in denominational name and in architecture. First Church stands like a fortress, towers marking the entrances. St. Paul's faces the world behind tall Grecian pillars. Bethel's horizontal structure gathers a large educational wing under an expanse of roof. Peace Church inherited a white-steepled building off Main Street a few years ago. Four churches, four names, four building styles—and four very different preachers.

Imagine that we can hear these preachers. It's Sunday morning and we are at a worship service led by Reverend Andrews. As we listen to his sermon we hear thoughtful ideas expressed in the measured cadence of a formal style. Quotations from noted authors indicate his range of reading. His vocabulary reveals him as a man of education. He bends over his manuscript, having written out the complete sermon; he delivers it almost word for word. He puts each word in its proper place, every sentence carrying a precise meaning. This controlled and thorough delivery depicts one style of preaching.

At St. Paul's the next Sunday, we see Dr. Brant, pastor of the congregation. The minister's warm smile and demeanor suggest kindness. He begins his message with a bit of humor, proceeds to make a point, illustrates it with a succession of stories, and continues to another thought loosely associated with the Scriptures. Comments on life and godliness are followed by another series of illustrations. He concludes with a heart-wrenching tale. His style contrasts markedly with that of the first preacher.

At Bethel, Mr. Carmichael's church, we hear yet

another kind of sermon. The pulpit vibrates with emotion. The preacher's rapid-paced message ranges from past to future in passionate language punctuated by peaks of excitement. He gestures vigorously as he travels the platform in long strides. We sense the preacher's deep feeling for his subject.

At Peace Church, Bill Dean demonstrates a novel preaching style. He drags a projector into the sanctuary. He illumines the front wall of the building with prepared slides. The outline of his message alternates with works of art and children's drawings. He's not afraid of the unusual gesture. While quoting one of the psalms he produces a flower pot from behind the lectern, lifts it above his head, and smashes it on the floor. His actions generate much discussion, and all but the custodian seem to enjoy his dramatic gesture.

These four styles radically diverge from one another. Yet each typifies a brand of better preaching in today's churches. These styles are far from ideal, but the unfortunate truth is that preaching fares much worse and sometimes fails to carry even into the first pew. At times that's because the preacher has little to say; on other occasions the preacher has something important to say, but doesn't know how to say it.

What would an ideal preacher sound like? How would he preach so that the message would penetrate the minds and hearts of people? Listen to one more preacher. This one has a vital message from the Scriptures to minister to the needs of his hearers. His sermon shows thoughtful organization and logical progression. In addition, he demonstrates stylistic techniques that allow his message to speak. He's clear: his word choice does not cloud the thought. He's captivating: his expressions and choice illustrations demand attention. More than that, he's penetrating: his language stirs the emotions. The pictures drawn by his word choice are powerful, his statements are phrased to linger. His conscious, thoughtful use of language propels the message to his listeners.

This, of course, is the ideal. But this ideal preacher can be as intimidating as he is inspiring. After all, how can an ordinary preacher learn to preach like this ideal? Most preachers don't practice their craft in a huge cathedral. Most don't teach homiletics in a seminary. And most preachers' sermons don't wind up on a bookshelf or on camera. How can reality approach this ideal?

The journey is circuitous, to be sure. We will begin with ancient orators and teachers of rhetoric. Then we will visit apostles and prophets. We'll also see church fathers and preachers throughout the ages. Even everyday preachers give us direction. Though circuitous, our path will lead us to our destination . . . a better preaching style.

Why bother with the trip? The Lord of the Word makes this undertaking important. Jesus said, "He who listens to you listens to me" (Luke 10:16). My hope is that this study will help the preacher proclaim the Lord's Word as clearly, as persuasively, and as powerfully as possible.

Part 1

Toward a Preaching Style

1

An Ancient Teacher

Perhaps it seems odd that the trip to better preaching starts in the classes on rhetoric taught by ancient scholars. A closer look at the principles of rhetoric, however, will show them to be invaluable to today's preacher. We'll learn from Aristotle in Athens, Quintilian in Rome, and several lesser lights.

The principles of rhetoric were the core of higher education in Greek and Roman schools. At that time, public speaking was a prerequisite for public life. The ability to speak well led to personal advancement and the opportunity to direct public opinion. So schools of rhetoric flourished.

Books, by contrast, were written reluctantly. Penned communication was thought either to serve a distant audience or to preserve the thoughts of an important speaker or teacher. Therefore speech held center stage in both the schools and the community. That was an oral age.

The Bible was written during this oral age, which explains not only some expressions but also the style of biblical writing. Much of Scripture is speech put on paper. The sometimes loosely structured statements of Scripture often contrast with modern books and the tightly organized sermon lifted word for word from a neatly typed manuscript.

ELEMENTS OF STYLE FOR PREACHING

Written style and oral style differ. The written page excels in accurately recording and preserving thoughts and ideas. For person-to-person communication, however, speech, is the best medium. Aristotle taught that the written style, though more finished and polished than oral, actually hinders the delivery of a speech.[1] The preacher like Reverend Andrews who values a manuscript should take notice.

The other preachers mentioned in the introduction also have something to learn from classical rhetoric, however. The teaching of rhetoric began when Greeks on the island of Sicily first formulated handbooks on the subject. When Gorgias, the character of Plato's dialogue by that name, brought rhetoric to Athens, it soon became a plaything of the dilettante. The Sophists, for example, developed rhetoric, defined its purpose as "persuasion," and taught that the art ought to appeal especially to the senses.

The Sophists stressed "successful" speaking and placed great emphasis on dazzling the audience. The disclaimer "mere sophistry" stems from their amoral use of the powers of persuasion. These speakers made ideas but pegs on which to hang gaudy colors of display. The thoughts of the speech were often no more important to the oration than a libretto may be to a florid operatic tenor.

Plato dismissed this sophistic excess as "cookery." His antagonism to the flowery manners of his day led to a style of speaking almost entirely focused on content. This reaction created a dry manner of speaking known as the "Attic" style.

A preacher's pride may send him down one or the other of these paths. If his intellectualism disdains any consideration of the language style of the sermon, he easily falls into Plato's error. But self-centeredness wears many suits. Another preacher may develop a speaking style designed to promote his reputation. For this minister, audience reaction determines success or failure. If people enjoy his sermon, he thinks he has succeeded. The string of stories designed to tug at the heart, the overly emotional sermon designed to excite people to their feet, and the dramatic presentation that leaves people exclaiming often reach into the Sophist's bag of tricks.

By gleaning Aristotle's works and Quintilian's *Institutes of Oratory*, the preacher learns of a balanced style of speaking that avoids self-centered ploys and places language firmly on the foundation of content. Quintilian described in detail the flamboyant styles that lack restraint. He said that too much attention to the niceties of style ruins speech. He also described the dry, Attic style and its lack of power, suggesting that style, like a sword, has power, but some speakers keep it permanently sheathed. The best style, he wrote, uses the tools of oratory in a natural and unaffected manner.[2]

Another important aspect of a good style is the use of figures of speech. Classical rhetoric didn't invent the figures; their use is as old as language itself. But ancient teachers did catalog these figures. Rhetoric defined and classified the figures of speech and made people conscious of their use.

Today's preacher can also benefit from understanding the three levels of style as offered by Aristotle, among others. The *plain*, or low, *style* characterizes itself: it's that style a speaker uses to communicate factual information. The style is unadorned and unemotional. When the speaker wishes to impress or persuade, however, he turns to the *middle style*. Although it may share some of the factual and logical content of the plain style, the middle style clothes it in a manner that catches the listener's attention. Vividness, energy, and an appropriate use of the figures of speech mark this level of style. The *high style* shows an abundance of ornamentation. In some hands the grand, high style became flowery; to modern ears it sounds overdone.

Teachers of rhetoric didn't draw these distinctions arbitrarily. They formulated these levels after listening to speeches. Even today, preachers and other speakers still use these levels of style. I suggest that all three may be and often should be heard in one sermon. Some speakers err, however, when they fail to think through their use of style and employ one or more of these levels inappropriately: what ought to be an urgent plea is stated in the matter-of-fact, plain style, while material that should be taught in a clear, controlled manner is delivered as if to warn people of a fire next door. Appropriate style is a key to effective speaking. If for no other reason than this, today's preacher ought to spend time with the ancient teachers to understand something of the three levels of style.

The subject of style held an honorable place in the classical age. Classical rhetoric divided into five categories: invention, arrangement, elocution (style), memory, and delivery.[3] Orators studied style; they drew principles from their research. How a matter must be stated received almost as much attention as the content or the arrangement of a speech.

Today "rhetoric" usually means "empty talk." One reason is this: the elocution movement, with its excessive emphasis on style, blossomed during the last century. As a result there currently exists a strong bias against style. The study of speech, especially style in speech, does not have high priority.

My goal is to show that the study of speech should have higher priority. We live in a time of electronic communication, when the importance of the spoken word is growing. Lessons from the oral age of the past have renewed value for speakers today. The subject of style is like a gold mine scarcely plundered and long neglected.

Style is not mere ornamentation; it is essential for effective communication. Set aside the bias against the subject, learn what's possible from classical rhetoric, and apply its principles in a thoughtful and biblical way to the most important kind of speaking this world will ever hear—preaching.

2

The Bible and Rhetoric

The argument up to this point is simple. Preaching is a rhetorical act, and the style of the sermon is a rhetorical issue. The wise preacher turns aside the prejudice against rhetoric and employs its principles in service to the sermon. This chapter has two aims: (1) to demonstrate that some principles taught by classical rhetoric can be found in Scripture, and (2) to show how the Bible itself employs style.

Some will question the use of classical rhetoric. Its origin in non-Christian thought, its checkered past, and its misuse at the hands of mere declaimers can be cited as reasons why the conscientious minister may not apply it to preaching. Should the preacher pluck the fruit of an art grown from pagan roots? Many argue that Paul's description of his own preaching seems to proclaim no.

> When I came to you, brothers, I did not come with eloquence or superior wisdom as I proclaimed to you the testimony about God. For I resolved to know nothing while I was with you except Jesus Christ and him crucified. I came to you in weakness and fear, and with much trembling. My message and my preaching were not with wise and persuasive words, but with a

> demonstration of the Spirit's power, so that your faith
> might not rest on men's wisdom, but on God's power
> (1 Cor. 2:1–5).

This passage is often interpreted to be a condemnation of any conscious use of stylistic techniques. Here's the reasoning behind that conclusion. Paul's use of the words "eloquence" and "persuasion" alludes to classical rhetoric. Although the art could be a tonic for weak preaching, the apostle in five short verses completely discredits it. Paul eschews eloquence. Even more strongly, he sets the Holy Spirit's power as antithetical to persuasive speech. Speaking that is Spirit-filled, then, cannot smack of style.

So goes the argument. But is this a valid conclusion? Does this passage really show that Paul opposes principles of good speech? Let's take another look.

The word translated "superior" in 1 Corinthians 2:1 contains the idea of excess.[1] Possibly Paul sets the power of the Spirit over against rhetorical excess rather than good speech. It is well within the realm of probability to think that Paul may have had his sights on the grandiose oratory practiced in his day.

A glance at the state of rhetoric during the first century A.D. shows a decline from the highest conceptions of the art. Both Longinus (first century A.D.) and Quintilian (c. A.D. 30–100) decry the existing low level of declaiming. Quintilian notes that Cicero (106–43 B.C.) suffered attacks by contemporaries who charged him with flamboyance.

Quintilian's contemporaries, however, considered Cicero dry. Perhaps political changes made the difference. As in Paul's day, there was totalitarian rule, which inclines a speaker to proclaim the expected. Creativity in such an environment tends toward augmented style rather than substance. Perhaps this is Paul's target. If so, we may risk the question, "Does the New Testament employ principles taught by classical rhetoric?"

There's some evidence that Luke may have been

acquainted with the rhetorical tradition. His writing shows rhetorical syllogisms[2] and the vocabulary of the tradition.[3]

Paul himself mentions that he uses a principle of rhetoric. He actually describes his own preaching as "persuasion" (2 Cor. 5:11). The evidence gains weight, moreover, when the literary structures and styles of the New Testament are examined.

First Corinthians 15 displays a framework that parallels the forensic speech outlined by classical rhetoric, even though it does not follow that form in every detail. Paul apparently dictated the letter and therefore that chapter (see 1 Cor. 16:21). Its oral style also betrays the forensic possibility. The chapter reads aloud easily and may represent the kind of persuasive speech Paul made on other occasions. It can stand alone, exhibiting a balanced structure recognizably like a lawyer's speech of the first century. Quintilian describes that speech form:

> In all forensic cases the speech consists of five parts, the *exordium* designed to conciliate the audience, the statement of facts designed to instruct him, the proof which confirms our own proposition, the refutation which overthrows the argument of the opponents, and the peroration which either refreshes the memory of our hearers or plays on their emotions.[4]

Paul comes close enough to this forensic speech form to evoke the courtroom for anyone familiar with that ancient idiom. Let's examine the structure of chapter 15 in this light.

The *exordium*, the introduction of a lawyer's speech, served to conciliate the judge and create a good relation between speaker and audience. The speaker often established an impression by a humility statement. He might describe the worth of the judge and the contrasting unworthiness of the speaker. Paul's introduction (vv. 1–2) is brief and to the point. He has little need to favorably dispose the reader to himself, for the chapter stands in the context of his letter written to a church he served. He focuses briefly on the message previously taught and urges upon the reader a continuance in the faith. Paul makes no statement of humility at this point.

The narration section (vv. 3–11) states the main facts of the resurrection. Paul cites two kinds of authority: the Scriptures and the witnesses. He provides names and numbers. He conforms to the format of the classical speech, which includes a statement of the facts of the case: the who, what, when, where, and how. At the end of this section he does include a humility statement. At this location it does not detract from the focus on the resurrection.

The exposition section of the forensic speech developed the main theme. Paul likewise expands upon the truth of resurrection (vv. 12–34) and counters the unbelief found within the church. He concludes the section with a brief personal appeal.

Paul follows the practice of a good lawyer, anticipating the argument of the opponent and raising questions before they are asked. The apostle, in a refutation section (vv. 35–49), begins, "But someone may ask . . . ," anticipating the thought of a skeptical Corinthian.

The *peroratio,* or conclusion, either recapitulated the speech or appealed to the emotions. Paul chooses the second option (vv. 50–58) and with memorable eloquence describes the sights and sounds of the resurrection. He rounds off the chapter with an echo of the introduction, reminding the reader to stand firm in the faith.

Did Paul study rhetoric? Does he consciously follow the classical form in this chapter? Although that question cannot be answered definitely, it's plain that Paul did not disdain recognizably good forms of speech. Whether he derived them from his culture, as is probable, or whether he arrived at them intuitively and independently matters little to the argument proposed.[5]

The evidence shows that Paul gave careful thought to the presentation of the message. He wrote and spoke persuasively because he put his mind to how it must be said. He either made use of rhetoric as he knew it or developed his own methods. I suspect that he consciously presented the subject of the resurrection using a known legal format to emphasize the truth of his teaching. It would hold up in court, he seems to imply. His example, in any case, can prod the preacher to give thought to how the message of God's Word could be presented.

Let's raise an objection. Even if Paul refers to sophistical excess in the first letter to the Corinthians, and although he presses forms into service similar to forensic speeches, this book is about preaching style rather than organization. Certainly the Scriptures show no interest in such a peripheral matter as style, do they?

In fact, they do. Early church fathers who were trained in rhetoric long ago discovered levels of style in Scripture. The three levels of style are present in 1 Corinthians 15. Notice the style in the narration section (vv. 3–11). Paul speaks of the central truths of the Christian faith clearly and simply. His phrases are short, he avoids figures of speech, his thought is unadorned and without emotion. This is an example of the plain style.

In the next section (vv. 12–34) Paul begins to persuade his reader. The subject matter remains much the same, but the purpose has changed. The style of his writing also changes. Notice how the "if" clauses pile up. Question follows question. Look at all the contrasts: faith and unbelief, Christ and Adam, life and death. Paul is not trying to display the skill of gaudy oratory; rather, he chooses a style that suits his purpose. Try to imagine Paul stating his argument in the matter-of-fact style of the previous section; it would lose force. Some preachers do that when their plain lecture style restrains what could be powerful persuasion.

When Paul anticipates the arguments of unbelief (vv. 35–49), he continues the middle style. Note his exclamations, the analogies, and the series of examples. He uses the second person, dialogue, and epigram. He builds another string of contrasts: First Adam and Last Adam; living, life giving; natural, spiritual; and variations on earth and heaven.

The conclusion brings still another style. Paul has

finished with analogy and example; the several contrasts are complete. Now he caps it all with an impassioned description of the glorious moment of resurrection. The short phrases sound the staccato note of the trumpet of victory.

A mighty crescendo begins with the imperative, "Listen." It's like music building for the grand theme. The periodic sentence in verse 54 saves its power for Isaiah's victory shout. Hosea's rhetorical questions, with death addressed by apostrophe ("O Death"), form the triumphal climax to which the apostle has been building. All this he aims directly at the reader by the use of the second person. He concludes the section with a song of victory over death. Having achieved the climax, he quickly lowers the pitch to the level at which he began. It's difficult to read these words without being carried along by the drama and emotion.

The language in this last section reveals the grand style. Try to read aloud the early verses of this chapter in the manner you naturally read the last verses—it seems wrong. Try to read the last section in the matter-of-fact manner of the first—it too is unnatural. Each style is appropriate to a purpose Paul has in mind.

Obviously the subject of style exists. The Scriptures also demonstrate levels of style. Perhaps we cannot be certain that the apostle Paul or other writers of Scripture consciously shifted from one style to another. Nevertheless, 1 Corinthians 15 does demonstrate levels of style. We learn from this chapter how style can serve content without hindering the flow of thought. Perhaps we begin to understand that a preacher's awareness of style, especially the levels of style, can indeed facilitate proclaiming God's Word.

Paul does not fear principles of speech. He uses them. Not only that, he uses them so well that the modern preacher can learn from his example. Whatever Paul intended when he disparaged eloquence in 1 Corinthians 2, his writing in chapter 15 demonstrates that he didn't oppose a wise use of principles of speech.

3

With What Language?

The golden age of Greece and the grandeur of both republican and imperial Rome bequeathed the tradition of rhetoric. Although the Scriptures emerged from a culture far removed from the centers of these societies, they exemplify principles taught by classical rhetoric. One reason for this could be that studying rhetoric is not prerequisite to using it. There may be another reason. Both Luke and Paul seem to use some of the words and forms associated with classical oratory. Although their example may encourage the preacher to adapt it to his work, a question remains. How can rhetorical principles of style be used without reverting to the self-serving tendencies that plagued so much of pagan oratory?

Preachers of the early church employed classical rhetoric. John Chrysostom, bishop of Constantinople beginning in A.D. 398, certainly did. His sermons abound with rhetorical devices. To our ears his sermons may seem overworked, but he lived in a different time. We live in the day of the book, the newspaper, and the written word (less so since the advent of radio and television). Chrysostom lived in the age of the spoken word, an oral age. The oratory of the theater gave people a standard. They expected the preacher to do as well as other speakers. Chrysostom measured up to their expectations.

Although examples of the use of rhetoric appear in the preaching of Chrysostom, among others, he left no organized homiletical discussion to guide preachers today in its use. For that there's another church father.

Augustine received rhetorical training as a youth from the declaimers he later denounced. After his conversion, he at first rejected rhetoric, complaining that its teachers concerned themselves with the law of letters and syllables while neglecting their own salvation. The whole rhetorical tradition is bound up with dishonesty, he declared. He later moderated his opinion.

> Now the art of rhetoric being available for the enforcing either of truth or falsehood, who will dare to say that truth in the person of its defenders is to take its stand unarmed against falsehood?[1]

> Now if anyone says that we need not direct men how or what they should teach, since the Holy Spirit makes them teachers, he may as well say that we need not pray, since our Lord says, "Your Father knoweth what things you have need of before ye ask him."[2]

Thus he urges rhetoric upon the preacher. But how can it best be used? How can rhetoric's long tradition concerning style help to advance the cause of God?

Augustine provides a solution in *On Christian Doctrine.* His book has two parts: how to understand the Scriptures, and how to communicate them. The first part deals with hermeneutics, and the second with homiletics. The second section contains the first good discussion of preaching and the best one seen for several centuries. In it Augustine rejects the sophistic attitude that content is unimportant. He also turns away from the exclusively material-centered approach advocated by Plato. Nevertheless, Augustine maintains the priority of content over form, since "wisdom is more important than eloquence."[3]

Augustine finds evidence for the Bible's use of rhetoric. He cites Romans 5:3–5 as an example of gradation or climax. Second Corinthians 11:16–30 contains periodic sentences. The three levels of style also appear in Scripture. First Corinthians 6:1–9 stands as an example of the elegant style, along with 2 Corinthians 6:2–10 and Romans 8:28–39. Romans 12:6–16 and especially Romans 13:12–14 employ the middle style. Augustine finds the plain style in Galatians 3:15–22.

Although the three levels of style can be found in Scripture, Augustine doesn't urge their use as displayed by speeches of classical orators, who tended to adapt the level of style to the subject matter. Augustine observes that the Bible uses the levels of style in unique ways. It modifies style to suit its purposes. The greatest change is in the Bible's applications of the grand style. It is not so much an ornate style of speaking, as with classical orators, but rather speech "exalted into vehemence by mental emotion."[4] The preacher can learn from that. Augustine doesn't think that a person preaching should be governed by just one style. Instead there should be a variety of styles used as long as they serve a good purpose.

What governs the use of these styles? Is it the content? Cicero taught, "He therefore will be eloquent who can speak of small things in a simple manner, of middling things in the intermediate style, and of great things in the grand manner."[5] Although Augustine has been called a Christian Cicero, he parts company with the Roman orator on this issue.

Augustine reads the Scriptures with an eye for styles and sees some interesting practices. For one thing, he notices that common matters sometimes call for a grand, impassioned manner of expression. Paul speaks in the high style in 1 Corinthians 6:1–8. The language moves the emotions. He desires change in the reader. Evidence of the high style is seen in sentences that come in short bursts. The contrasts are striking, questions pile up, the language style goes beyond metaphor and ornament, question and statement alternate—

all marks of this style. But look how ordinary the subject matter is! He speaks of people taking each other to court. That common legal matters call for such a vehement statement is out of place, according to classical teaching.

Why does Paul employ a grand style when speaking of plain, everyday matters? Augustine's answer is this:

> In questions like ours, however, where all things, and especially those addressed to the people from the place of authority, ought to have reference to men's salvation, and that not their temporal but their eternal salvation, and where the thing to be guarded against is eternal ruin, everything that we say is important.[6]

The legal actions of Corinthian Christians are important and call for the grand, impassioned style of speech because their life as a church and their witness is at stake. Everything we say is important. The subject of a cup of cold water is important. Is Augustine saying that preachers should speak in the high manner at all times because all matters are important? Not at all. In his study of Scripture he finds another divergence from classical norms when the Scriptures speak of great matters.

> Is there anything greater than God Himself? Is nothing then to be learned about Him? Or ought he who is teaching the Trinity in unity to speak of it otherwise than in the method of calm discussion, so that in regard to a subject which is not easy to comprehend, we may understand as much as it is given us to understand?[7]

Augustine clearly advocates speaking of the greatest of subjects in a plain teaching style. These principles gleaned from Scripture lead preaching onto a road not traveled by classical orators. They considered speaking of sublime matters in the plain style a terrible fault.

Erich Auerbach coins a helpful expression to describe Augustine's approach. He calls it *sermo humilis*. The word *sermo* is larger than the English word "sermon," though it is its root. It means "speech" or "language." *Humilis* enters our vocabulary as "humility" and "humus." "Humus" is a gardener's word denoting soil rich in organic material. *Sermo humilis* is "humble language," or perhaps "down-to-earth speech."

Auerbach traces the separate roads traveled by the developing Christian church and the declining Roman culture. The Bible remained a foreign piece of literature to the cultivated Roman. Those with an ear and eye for the classical Latin style looked down on the supposed crudities found in the Scriptures, especially in the Latin translation. The residual Hebraisms, the Greek expressions, and the lack of a cultivated manner of expression offended the educated elite. Words like *salvator, mediator, redemptio, spiritualis*, and others the classicist deemed wooden and clumsy. But these were (and are—they need no translation) words dear to the heart of the Christian.

The humble style of the Scriptures did not bother the common person, many of whom could not read. They heard these words gladly. The church grew and multiplied because the common people heard the message in plain words and in their own tongue.

But what does this say for the three styles? Does it mean that the most effective speech comes only in the lowly plain style? A look at Augustine's own style provides an answer. Although he spoke in the plain, unadorned style at times, he did not fear a more elevated manner when it suited a purpose. Auerbach describes the style as demonstrated in Augustine's book *The Trinity*. There is

> the dramatic ascent from the lowly world, which remains present even when Augustine rises, carrying his readers with him, to heights of ecstasy and abstraction, the furious urgency of his plea, in which all theory seems forgotten, the direct appeal to the reader, whoever he may be—all these shatter every barrier between you and me: such a style level would have been almost inconceivable at an earlier day.[8]

Although Augustine freely employs the various levels of style, he's careful to write in a manner that speaks to the reader. His preaching is the same. His homiletic understands the classical tradition, but he does not seek to polish language just to please the sophisticated. He's willing to bend and break classical rules to speak plainly and persuasively to common folk.

So Augustine's discussion in *On Christian Doctrine* and the example of his preaching and writing provide a key to the best use of classical teachings on style. His discussion reflects the temper of the church in his time, but more than that. It echoes something of his own experience of radical conversion from the halls of the elite to the clapboards of the church. Even more than that it demonstrates a biblical theme.

Paul's beautiful hymn of the humble Savior (Phil. 2:1–11) portrays the Christ emptying himself. God gave his Son, born a frail infant, to the arms of a young girl, to a carpenter's home. Jesus was materially poor. He did not consort with the elite. He was removed culturally from the centers of power and learning. He came to serve in loving obedience to the Father. His faithfulness led to an ignoble, crude, and cruel death on a Roman cross. This Jesus God has exalted highly and is the Lord proclaimed by his heralds today. This grand theme of Christ emptying himself provides the best content for that word *humilis*.

The wise preacher also leaves the halls of elitism with its dry intellectualism. And he avoids the pitfall of overreaction marked by cute sophistries. He speaks with humus on his tongue. The great and difficult teachings he explains in clear and common language. Yet he's not afraid to persuade or to lift people to great heights and mobilize them for action by that purposeful and sometimes furious style urged by and demonstrated by Augustine.

4

The Scholastic Sermon

A professor preaches a sermon sometime during the last half of the thirteenth century. The place is probably a chapel at the University of Paris. A congregation of students, teachers, and priests gathers to hear a sermon delivered by the greatest philosopher of the time, Thomas Aquinas. The text he uses on this Palm Sunday is Matthew 21:5, a quotation from Zechariah 9:9, the prophecy of "the humble King." Although his native tongue is an early form of Italian and the congregation speaks mostly French, Thomas intones his sermon in Latin.

Aquinas's preaching shows a standard form. The sermon begins with the prayer—actually a call to prayer, such as "Pray the Lord, therefore, that by the power of spiritual teaching today your hearts may be uplifted." It moves on to the *protheme*, or introduction to the theme. The preacher then announces his theme, typically based on the Scripture reading for the day. He also announces three divisions, the number reflecting the doctrine of the Trinity. The fifth section contains the content of the sermon and shows great sophistication and much elaboration. A conclusion caps the message.[1]

ELEMENTS OF STYLE FOR PREACHING

In Aquinas's sermon, entitled "The Coming of the King," the three divisions are "dignity, utility, and manner." It develops in an elaborate, intellectually sophisticated manner; the first two divisions contain seven points each, and the third has four points.

Aquinas is preaching his sermon at a time of theological ferment and change. The influence of the classical era shows in the theology of the day and in the content of the sermons. Aristotle's logic has greatly influenced thinking and preaching, but his writing on rhetoric has not. Neither has classical rhetoric as a whole had much influence on this formal style of preaching. The sermon's organization has not come from ancient time. There is no evidence of the five parts of a classical oration. But the structures show a knowledge of Aristotle's logical categories.

The light of Augustine's homiletical teaching fails to shine on the scholarly sermon of the Middle Ages. His direct style of speaking cannot be found here. Some of the preaching handbooks indicate that his work is known. But his principles of style fail to influence preaching. Instead of a style of speech aimed at the listener, the sermon shows the lofty style of the scholar. There's no message for the common folk with this style.

Something happened beginning two centuries before the occasion of Thomas's Palm Sunday sermon. Latin had been in decline, and native tongues gradually replaced it. In the eleventh century, however, scholars discovered a new use for the Roman tongue. Since its dormant state froze the meaning of words and expressions, it provided the scholar, scientist, and theologian with a language of specialization. Students from various countries, language groups, and the many dialects had a vehicle for universal communication. For several centuries, at least for the learned, a universal language transcended the tongues of the nations. That scholars spoke to scholars in a language beyond the masses influenced preaching.

Preaching mirrored the division of language. Some preached *ad populum* to common folk in the vernacular. But the preacher in the monastery and especially at the university not only spoke in Latin, but used a style and content that has been called *ad clerum*. One type of sermon for the people and another, the more creative and illustrious of the two, appeared side by side. Aquinas's sermon was definitely *ad clerum*.

No, not all sermons preached in the thirteenth century were *ad clerum*. Perhaps most were not. A few miles from the university the congregation of the village church heard the other sermon style, if the priest thought it necessary to preach. Few *ad populum* sermons have been preserved; few were worth printing. Consequently this style contributes little to the preaching of later times. Those that made it into print are mostly verse-by-verse explanations of the Bible. Bad examples contain messages on the lives of the saints, and the worst try to amuse in the fashion of an after-dinner speech.

The three-point sermon comes from the scholastic age of Aquinas and demonstrates the durability of preaching traditions. It lives on even though consciousness of the Trinitarian motivation has mostly disappeared. Yet other medieval traditions persist. Forming divisions of a sermon by applying categories (often Aristotle's) continues, and that has a deadly effect on preaching style. The Latin of the sermon also seeps into present times. Some preachers use a churchly language distinguished from everyday speech. The language of the church shows more Latin-derived words, more archaic words, and more of scholarly language than the speech of business or social conversation. Although this distinct style of speech does not differ as radically as Latin differed from thirteenth-century vernaculars, the tendency is there and it colors many sermons.

So the *ad clerum* tendency lives on. Those attempts to dazzle by a display of intellect, fine distinctions, and abstract speculations are faithful to the tradition. A common complaint against preachers is that they preach to fellow preachers with professors looking over their shoulder: blame it on the *ad clerum* sermon of the Middle Ages.

5

The Influence of Ramus

Luther and Calvin turned aside from the complex, scholastic, Latin sermons of the Middle Ages. Luther's preaching belongs to Luther. A comparison of his sermons with the preaching of the Middle Ages shows a disdain for the rigid form of the latter. Luther forged his method and style of preaching in the foundry of struggle, with the hammer and anvil of necessity, out of the fire of opposition. His vivid style is unmistakable. Listen to him preach on Jesus' presentation in the temple:

> God gives them this Child and He is to them a stone of stumbling and a sign of offense. The text relates that when Mary and Joseph brought Jesus into the Temple only two persons were there out of a populous city. Is it not shocking that from more than twenty thousand men only Simeon should be present? The priests pocketed the five groschen and paid no more attention to the Child. Is it not shameful? Ought not half the town at least have come out to see the Lord of all the world? But because there was no pomp, no one gave heed and Mary and Joseph brought Him in alone. None but Simeon and Anna were there. So it is today in the

world, and even among Christians. If it were only the Turks, the Jews, and the mad princes it would be bearable, but we Christians are the ones who despise Him. The pope, the bishops, the fanatics, peasants, townsmen, nobles tread Him underfoot, and I do it myself. I cannot believe in Him as I should. He ought to be my true friend and comforter. But the "old donkey" in me won't have it, and the devil blows the bellows. In my heart it is just as bad as it is in the world. He is a sign to be spoken against.[1]

Luther returned to an Augustinian style and spoke plainly and forcefully. But his understanding of the principles of preaching did not ripen into an organized viewpoint. He left no homiletical guideline behind other than scattered comments and the example of his sermons. His followers replaced his loose but vigorous style with its opposite, the dry scholastic manner.

Calvin turned to the ancient homily as a model for his preaching method. He cited a phrase or a verse of Scripture and then proceeded to explain it. His method betrayed the teacher that he was. His virtues of style helped overcome in part the limitation of this method. Calvin spoke in plain language with remarkable clarity. He added a bit of spice to his sermons through homely metaphors and pithy sayings. His words carried into the pulpit the sights, smells, and tastes of daily life. Listen to him preach on Ephesians 2:8–10:

How now? they argue. Shall we not be saved by our own merits and by our good works? And where do you get them from? says St. Paul. Have you coined them in your own shop, or have you some garden planted by yourself from which to gather them, or do they spring, I do not know how, from your own labors and skill, so that you may advance yourselves by them? No, for on the contrary, you know that God has prepared them. And is it fitting that you should go about raising objections against him, when he has pitied you and shown himself bountiful towards you? Is it becoming

> that you should presume to step forward to pay him,
> and to say that you have money of your own?[2]

A reading of Calvin's sermons shows a pulpit ability far stronger than his reputation admits. Gone were the fine distinctions of scholasticism. He turned aside from much of the intellectualism, the dry explanations, and the remote style that wearied the listener. In its place Calvin put a clarity of expression punctuated by interesting examples, questions, analogies, dialogue, and direct address that reasoned with the hearer.

Like Luther, Calvin failed to leave a systematic study of principles of preaching. His followers scrambled for some kind of method. In the Calvinistic wing of the Reformation, scholastic methods surged to fill in the gap. One who rode the crest of the wave was Ramus.

Peter Ramus was born in 1515 in northern France. He came from a family of modest means, but managed to secure a good education. His fame grew as a logician and a reformer of educational methods. He wrote more than sixty widely used books on logic and philosophy and coauthored thirteen works with his colleague, Taleus.

Ramus's philosophy focused on order. He assumed that a simple and understandable order filled the universe. The world, he thought, is a copy of an ordered hierarchy of ideas existing in the mind of God. To logic is given the task of describing how things follow one another in nature. If the account holds true, then we can safely act on it.

Ramus laid out the pattern of ideas in such a way that a diagram of logic with divisions and subdivisions formed a blueprint of the universe. He put the system on paper, charting the logical flow from general categories to the specific. Every distinction on his chart was an either/or, such as inductive/deductive, genus/species, primary/secondary, and discrete/continuous. Logic itself divides into individual ideas/doctrines. Individual ideas are either established by experience or rest on a witness's authority. Such logical pairing signals the method of Ramus.

Thinking, according to this Ramian method, means the unveiling of the ideal form best done by pairing every idea with its counterpart. Though he claimed to present a system to replace the fascination with Aristotle that characterized the Middle Ages, his chart shows many similarities to the Greek philosopher's logical and topical writings. He derived some of his categories from Aristotle, and the pairings also resemble some of his arrangements.

Ramus examined the ancient systems of philosophy and rhetoric. Classical logic organized into two divisions: invention and disposition. Rhetoric was arranged into five departments: invention, disposition, style, delivery, and memory. A duplication occurred in these categorizations that violated Ramus's logical method, however, and he felt that both fields couldn't claim the same territory. Invention and disposition must be a part of either logic or rhetoric and cannot belong to both, he decided. So he did something that paid consequences for years to come.

He assigned the matters of invention and disposition to logic and gave the subjects of style and delivery to rhetoric. That greatly reduced the field of rhetoric compared with classical schemes. The subject called "memory" got lost in the revision but was theoretically related to logic.

This arrangement put a distance between what is said—the content—and how it is said—the style. Accordingly, style, like frosting on the cake, makes the content palatable. Style serves as decoration. The content of the speech is all important. The arrangement of the materials of the speech in a logical (Ramian) manner retains high priority. But consideration of the manner in which the materials are presented becomes peripheral to consideration of the content or arrangement.

Taleus then developed the now limited area of rhetoric, divorced from the content and the arrangement of a speech. He defined rhetoric as the art of speaking well. He divided rhetoric into two parts (remember that Ramian arrangement comes in pairs): style and delivery. He subdivided style into tropes and figures; delivery comprised voice and gesture.

With his emphasis on the tropes (words used in nonstandard ways) and figures as the main substance of rhetoric, Taleus endorsed the view that good style is a flight from the natural. Speaking well means a use of figures accompanied by an appropriate delivery. A sentence arranged in an ordinary manner is ineffective. Rhetoric demands an elevated speech, that is, a charming use of ornaments and striking expressions. Style, now divorced from content, merely plucks flowers from the garden of eloquence to brighten the table.

On the one hand, Ramian logic shows a too convenient, too orderly, too simple analysis that can be charted on paper. On the other hand, Taleus's rhetoric accentuates frosting and flowers. The separation strongly influenced the preaching of the sixteenth and seventeenth centuries. Some sermons showed a stark arrangement of content in a highly logical sequence, while others used words as colorful display.

Two events helped propel Ramian ideas into prominence among Protestants. The first was Ramus's conversion from Roman Catholicism to Protestantism in 1562. The second occurred ten years later on St. Bartholomew's Day in Paris; Ramus suffered martyrdom on the third day of the massacre.

In England, the Ramian brand of logic and rhetoric triumphed over other schools of thought. Although the influence of classical rhetoric continued, the majority of handbooks on rhetoric written in the sixteenth and seventeenth centuries showed the influence of Ramus. "School boys were taught by their Ramist masters that the knowledge of the three simple rules of method made them masters of the complexities of all logical structure—in an oration or poem . . . quite as much as in any scientific treatise."[3] The education of many a Puritan included the logic of the French philosopher Ramus and the rhetoric of his friend Taleus. Their sermons showed the influence.

The Puritan preachers spoke in what they called "the plain style." In contrast to the ornamental eloquence of Anglican preaching, or the interesting, witty presentations of others, the Puritans emphasized logical clarity. "Painted, obscure sermons, like the painted glass in the windows that keeps out light, are too often the works of painted hypocrites," said Richard Baxter. "The paint upon the glass may feed the fancy, but the room is not well lighted by it."[4] The plain style of the Puritans emphasized clarity, conveyed first by a logical and orderly presentation and only then by the possible addition of metaphor and example.

Puritan sermons had typically a fourfold structure. The first was the text, a passage of Scripture, usually brief, announced to the congregation and "opened" by explaining the author, the occasion, and the context. Second, from the text the preacher deduced certain doctrinal propositions and announced them, sometimes assigning each a number. The third part gave the "reasons" for the doctrine. In this phase several passages of the Bible were analyzed as authority to support the reasons and then their truth was represented by example. This method "proved" the doctrines stated. All this addressed the mind of the listener.

In the fourth and most practical part of the sermon, the preacher abruptly shifted to the "uses." He milked the doctrines of many applications. Here, finally, he had an opportunity to address the will of the people and to move them to act upon the teaching they heard. The method was predictable. The listeners knew what was coming. If they had a decent memory, they could repeat a digest of the sermon. Some of the people took notes, transferring the logically stated ideas to paper.

Thomas Hooker, a Puritan leader in the colonies and founder of the city of Hartford, Connecticut, preached a sermon entitled "The Soul's Exaltation," based on 1 Corinthians 6:17.[5] His approach to preaching illustrates the Puritan method and the Ramian influence upon it.

Hooker's introduction recapitulates previous sermons in a series. In it he states that the application of the merits of Christ consists especially in two things. He announces the two and proceeds to subdivide the second into two parts. The second subdivision is again divided. He follows that pattern of analyzing what he said in previous sermons through two more subdivisions until he comes to the statement of the doctrines. He finds two doctrines in the text. The first is that every believer is joined to Christ; the second is that he is so joined that he becomes one spirit with Christ. He then supports the two doctrines with reasons or arguments. He usually arranges the reasons in pairs, although he breaks the pattern occasionally. The reasons contain appeals to Scripture and examples. The sermon up to this point is tightly arranged and can be charted. Hooker then moves to the uses.

Hooker extrapolates five applications from the doctrines established. They are as follows: (1) union with Christ is a privilege; (2) the doctrine warns those who persecute the Christian that they persecute Christ; (3) the teaching provides a basis for self-examination in asking whether or not we are united to Christ; (4) it provides a ground of consolation, first in the face of opposition, and second, in temptation; (5) if we are united to Christ we must walk worthy of the calling.

The Puritan sermon had visible strengths. It attempted to be loyal to the Word of God. It also revealed thoughtfulness and a varied vocabulary. Some preachers had no fear of a strong statement. Henry Scougal said, "The vulgar that . . . sit under the pulpit are commonly as hard and dead as the seats they sit on."[6] Only strong language can pierce.

But the Puritans forsook oral style with its directness and power of communication. They turned away from the ear of the congregation by an appeal to the eye: by a visual arrangement of the subject and by the language of the treatise. The sermons were not so much a cry of the herald, nor the deliverance of an ambassador, but the instruction manual of a stern, demanding teacher. The Word of God moved off center—in spite of the text and appeals to scriptural authority. The Bible as presented by Puritan method became an object of study, a subject of analysis, a field in which the divine order may be discovered. The order disclosed, however, resembled Ramian categories.

The Methodists also drank from the Ramian well. Walter J. Ong argues that the very name of the movement came from the method of logic taught by Ramists.[7] John Wesley's *Compendium of Logic* with its dichotomies reveals such an influence.

Ramian influence entered the Americas by at least two avenues, the Puritan and the Methodist movements. Traces of Ramus's influence remain; countless sermons can be found that are essentially a doctrinal analysis of a text. The custom of dividing the sermon into exposition and application as distinct and separate parts continues into the twentieth century. The practice of what may be called "great leap preaching"—preaching that jumps from doctrinal teaching to practical matters or from the biblical era to the present—lingers. It asks, "Now, how does all this apply to our situation today?" That leap is rooted in the distinction between doctrine and uses that was practiced by the Puritans. It also stands as an obstacle to an effective, concrete style of preaching.

The obscure French logician has left a legacy. The lowly place given style in speech today stems in part from Ramus's truncated rhetoric. When you hear a preacher separate doctrine and practice, or divorce content from style, you have been given part of Ramus's estate. When you hear a sermon weakened by the style of the printed page, forsaking the power possible in speech for a distinctly written manner, it is the sixteenth-century manner still at work today.

6

Some Modern Influences on Sermon Style

Scholasticism's long arm reaches into many twentieth-century sermons. Its fingers touch both the content and the style of preaching. Although it still influences the language of some sermons, other—often more powerful—movements can color the message preached today.

Consider the following scenario. A preacher noted for clarity and precision, who normally leaves the listener with little doubt about his thought, preaches on immortality. He says this: "But underneath and overhead and through this present life, like sunshine which one does not always think of but which is here, runs a strong conviction that vivifies and illumines and dignifies everything, that spiritual life is eternal and that ahead of it the doors are open. That is all we need to know, that ahead the doors are open."[1]

In spite of simile and metaphor, tools that usually make truth vivid, the expression presents vague generalities. What does it mean that the doors are open? A comparison of this excerpt with several biblical descriptions of eternal life shows a striking contrast. Why does a preacher, famous for his ability to communicate concretely, slip into a vague manner of expression?

Here is another example from a different source and direction. "The religious response, on the other hand, would be to look at the Resurrection out of the corner of the eye rather than directly, to catch the mystery and the wonder of it."[2] How do you look at something out of the corner of your eye? He speaks figuratively. One way of reading the message of the Scriptures looks between the words, the statements, the descriptions, and the explanations. If the truth lies between words, then it is not clear, understandable language that matters. Such a reading of the Bible can favor the opaque expression evoking mystery and other-worldliness.

Why do some speak vaguely? The answer lies in the way people think. There is a system of thought that exerts as large an influence today as Ramian logic did on the Puritans. Immanuel Kant created a philosophical distinction that hangs over contemporary thinking and preaching. Simply put, he divided reality into two realms: the phenomenal and the nomenal. The first is the world of nature and science; the second speaks of morality and religion. The world we experience dwells on the one side; on the other, the world beyond sense experience. Between the two stands what can be called Kant's "picket fence."

That fence has no gate and marks a boundary line through the thinking of some philosophers, scientists, theologians, and yes, preachers. People who ponder the issues and problems of the world, who are overly influenced by these notions, take a stand on one side or the other of that fence.

Some, setting their feet on the phenomenal side of the pickets, assume that truth comes to the senses only. According to this scheme, what cannot be seen, heard, or verified by any other sense either doesn't exist or doesn't matter much.

This is a recipe for doubt. Who has seen God? Who carries him into the laboratory? If he's not palpable, is he really there at all? The secular mind betrays this stance. More devastatingly, some preachers do too. But they expose their viewpoint in sermons that focus largely on this world, on

man, on society, on what can be seen and h
preaching is almost embarrassed by the thou
beyond. So it speaks of eternity only by figure ͗
mism.

Other thinking and preaching jump to the opposite side
of the fence. Truth is feeling, it is poetry, and it calls forth a
faith divorced from facts of history. When truth is thought to
lie outside history, then preaching is embarrassed by such
matters as the Bible's narrative of the Resurrection.

This second stance presents a mountain-sized problem
for the preacher. How can anyone communicate what is
essentially a mystery, what is beyond seeing and hearing, in
words designed to vibrate the air in the realm of sense? It's
impossible. Yet it is hoped that by stretching and straining,
perhaps by using language that evokes mystery and paradox, a message gets through.

Tendencies in preaching can fall in either of these two
directions. Either faith finds its focus in a man-centered
world of the here and now, or faith retreats before the
encroachments of skeptical science to a realm on the other
side of the fence beyond the senses. The first tendency tries
to limit preaching to this world's affairs, while the second
one strains to speak of what is wholly other.

The second tendency is the more recent. The first
belongs to a dated liberalism, although some discover it
anew. The problem presented to the preacher by the second
scheme can be illustrated in a story told by J. D. Crossan.[3]

Crossan forsakes the realm of science for the world of
poetry and feeling. He tells a story of the lighthouse and its
keeper. There's land and there's sea. On land stands a
lighthouse, and at sea float rafts of land-based materials. In
the lighthouse is the keeper. People bob along on the rafts at
sea. The keeper knows the people, even if all the people
don't know him. Communication flows between the keeper
and the people so that they can be guided safely home to
land. According to Crossan, that's precisely the view the
Bible presents—an old-fashioned view.

One day something happened. The rumor grew that

land didn't exist. If there isn't any land, then there can't be a lighthouse; without a lighthouse there can be no keeper. All that's real is the people on rafts bobbing on the restless sea. Crossan regards the rafts as representing language. So it's people and language, or people and their story, nothing more.

What about God? Crossan's reasoning runs this way. If God is identified with the raft, there's an idol. Since God can't be identified with language, he doesn't reveal himself in the message of the Bible. He's beyond the edge of language, if indeed he's out there somewhere. Perhaps he's somehow identified with the sea. If not, "there is only one possibility left, and that is what we can experience in the movement of the raft, in the breaks in the raft's structure, and what can be experienced at the edges of the raft itself."[4] Especially at the edges of the raft of language can a person find some hint of what may be beyond in the unknown and silent realm. What's the language of the edges? It's the language of wonder, of mystery, of paradox, of looking at the Resurrection out of the corner of the eye.

Preaching built on such assumptions wants a style of language that's purposefully vague. Words are chosen for their ability to create an aura and to stir the emotions. It demands a rhetoric of mystery. Clear, straightforward exposition of the Scriptures cannot stand on such assumptions.

How different is the biblical message:

> That which was from the beginning, which we have heard, which we have seen with our eyes, which we have looked at and our hands have touched—this we proclaim concerning the Word of life (1 John 1:1–2).

John's testimony of Jesus shows no evidence of modern distinctions. It gives no support to Kant's picket fence. What John tells us assumes that the fence isn't there. He also informs us that the lighthouse stands. John knows the keeper. John has seen him. John has heard him. John shook his hand. John walked with him and talked with him. John calls the keeper "the Word." He bears that name because the keeper reveals God's light to people. As part of his apostolic task, John speaks and writes of the Son of God whose sandals raised dust on the byways of Israel.

Paul likewise presents the gospel as a mystery made known (Eph. 3:3). God entrusted him with an administration of mystery, and his preaching communicated it. He didn't keep the revelation mysterious or make it more mysterious. Although the deep doctrines of God remain incomprehensible, and no one can measure the pinnacle of truth, nevertheless, Paul always sought to make all matters plain.

A style of preaching built on biblical assumptions seeks to communicate the gospel of Jesus Christ as directly, as powerfully, and as urgently as possible. Such preaching doesn't focus on the edges of language, nor does it want to hide glorious truths behind vague statements. In both content and style it seeks to make clear to people what is the revealed Word of God.

One's philosophy and theology affect style. That should serve notice that the matter of style neither stands alone nor hangs on the periphery. The preacher's assumptions about God, creation, and revelation as well as the purpose and task of preaching all affect choices of style. Modern assumptions ask for a rhetoric of mystery. Biblical assumptions demand a down-to-earth style.

Part 2

A Theory of Style

7

A Theory of Style

The pursuit of style in preaching has led along a winding path. Ancient rhetoric, biblical example, Augustinian theory, scholastic retreat, and modern doubt have marked the way. This section ties strands gathered from past and present to form a theory of style. It also serves as a transition to a discussion of the elements of a preaching style found in the third part of this book.

What is preaching? To make good style choices in preaching, the pastor must have the full view of what his task requires. Preaching brings a message from the Scriptures, God's Word, to the church and the world. The servant of the Word stands under the authority of Scripture and proclaims its truth. Preaching demands the power of the Holy Spirit. Good preaching also calls for a preacher steeped in the Scriptures and sensitive to the needs of people.

Nevertheless, when the preacher chooses how, in what manner, to bring the message to a particular audience, he wades deeply into questions of style. What guidance does he have in these choices? Rhetorical principles shaped by preaching's distinctive task.

Let me summarize what we learned from rhetoric.

Classical rhetoric distilled, among other insights, the three levels of style. When we listen to preachers and other speakers today, we can still hear these styles at work. That they serve a purpose even today validates the analysis of the ancient teachers of rhetoric.

The Scriptures, both the Old and New Testaments, offer examples of the use of rhetorical principles. Prophets and apostles employed schemes and tropes in their preaching and writing as well as levels of style. The three levels of style, however, appear in Scripture in a unique way. Rather than importing the high style unaltered, with its grand, self-serving manner, the Scriptures adapt this style to a higher purpose. The focus changes from decoration to emotion.

Augustine developed preaching theories against the backdrop of Roman rhetorical excess. His distinctive contributions grew out of the example of biblical writers. We too can weave the three levels of style to suit our purposes in preaching.

The knot that ties the strands together is *intention*. Why does the preacher speak in a certain manner? To what end does he employ one style or another? Why does he string rhetorical questions together at this point in his sermon, or why does he now give an example? Every preacher makes style choices; they can't be avoided. Since the sermon will show some kind of style, why not make conscious, intelligent, and helpful choices? But what guidelines govern such selections? Should he preach with one style, or should he incorporate the others? Only when the preacher knows *what* he must do in a sermon can he decide *how* he will do it. Intention directs the preacher in this choice.

What is intention? Preaching betrays any of three intentions. The sermon may be designed to instruct, to persuade, or to move to respond. Better sermons often display some combination of these three. If the intent is to instruct people as to the meaning of a passage, there's a suitable style. If it's reasoning with people to persuade them of the validity of a teaching or of its importance, there's a style made for such a purpose. Is the intent to move people

to commitment or action? Again, there are stylistic consider-
ations to make.

What shapes a preacher's intention? What signals the
need for instruction, for example? Preachers look in two
directions for guidance. First they look at Scripture. The
passage chosen as a basis for the sermon presents a certain
style. It also makes certain demands on the sermon and its
style.

For example, some passages cry out for instruction.
Think of preaching on John 10:34–38. Jesus was debating
with people ready to stone him. Why? That needs explanation. He spoke of gods and of the law; he quoted a psalm; he
emphasized the authority of Scripture—all demanding explanation. A sermon on Proverbs 30:8, by contrast, may need
but a little instruction on the meaning of poverty and riches.
The passage calls for language that persuades people and
moves them toward contentment. Ephesians 3:20–21 points
to a different intention. Although some matters in that
passage may need a brief explanation, the text itself offers a
song of praise. The doxological style of the passage
influences a sermon on it. So the Scripture passage guides
the preacher's intention.

Preachers also look to the people for cues. Their hopes
and needs shape the purpose. How much instruction do
they require? Is your audience from the university or the
factory? Is your church inner-city black or suburban white?
Although about fifteen percent of Americans are college
graduates, a degree is no guarantee of thoughtfulness or
knowledge of the Bible. Some people need more instruction
than others. Some need to be persuaded, while others may
already be convinced of a truth. The audience may be
skeptical or overflowing with faith. They may have traveled a
short or long distance on the path of obedience. Will you
address the mind, the imagination, or the will of the listener?
Good preaching takes aim before it lets the arrow fly.

A sermon may have a primary intention, such as
instruction, with other purposes interwoven. A sermon
whose main aim is to teach may also wish to persuade

people of the value of the teaching and to move them to act upon it.

Three kinds of intention, we noted, can commonly be found in sermons: teaching, persuading, and moving. Speaking styles, likewise, fall into three levels: low, middle, and high. An inner connection joins the level of style and the intent of the preacher. One style serves instruction best. Another level of style helps persuasion. The third level tends to move people. Given their purposes, let's rename the levels of style. Instead of calling them low, middle, and high, let's with an eye to a preacher's intention, label them *a teaching style, a persuading style,* and *a moving style.*[1]

Take a closer look at these three styles. Each includes a combination of elements or qualities. The five elements of style are the following: *clarity, interest, evocative language* (for lack of a better word I call this quality "evocation"), *energy,* and *emotion* (see part 3). Each element can be described by certain characteristics of language. For example, the characteristics that promote the element of energy in a speech include vividness, simplicity, variety, active verbs, the present tense, shorter sentences, and the second person (see chap. 11).

These characteristics I have labeled "aspects" of a preaching style, using the word *aspect* in the sense of "component part." A wise use of these aspects of style gives a sermon a certain quality, such as, in the example used, energy.

What connection do these elements and aspects of style have to the three major levels of style?

THE TEACHING STYLE

Consider the teaching style. It emphasizes clarity, the first element of a good style. Plainly stated, clear (not vague or obscure) words and phrases are the heart of this style. Simple expressions, specific language, descriptive phrases, and a little repetition when necessary help to clarify ideas. Short, concrete words and the absence of jargon, unconventional language, and abstract words contribute to clarity, a major element of a good teaching style.

A teaching style need not be dull. Preachers ought to make their teaching interesting (another element of a good preaching style). As they bring biblical teaching to the people they can do so in a delightful, arresting manner by adding the spice of interest. Preachers do not need to avoid the other elements of style when they instruct. These other elements usually remain in the background, however, for if misused or overused they can compete with that primary element of clarity. For an example, slipping into a figure of speech when a precise statement is called for gives the message a "mushy" texture. The teaching style has something of the character of the low style of classical rhetoric. It can be visualized like this:

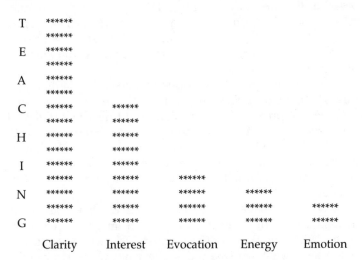

T	******			
	******			
E	******			
	******			
A	******			
	******			
C	******	******		
	******	******		
H	******	******		
	******	******		
I	******	******		
	******	******	******	
N	******	******	******	******
	******	******	******	******	******
G	******	******	******	******	******
	Clarity	Interest	Evocation	Energy	Emotion

THE PERSUASIVE STYLE

A sermon limited to teaching, however, may fail to reach an important biblical goal. The better preacher strives to persuade people. A clear presentation of biblical truth builds the necessary foundation for persuasion, but by itself is not always so effective. Besides, some people are aware of a teaching but are not persuaded of its importance. So good preaching will attempt to reach as deeply into the mind and the heart of the listener as language can. That demands a persuasive style.

This goal in no way competes with the persuasive activity of the Holy Spirit. Without the Spirit's power, the preaching of God's Word leaves the listener indifferent at best. "Why is my language not clear to you? Because you are unable to hear what I say," said Jesus (John 8:43). Spiritual indifference and rebellion present the preacher with obstacles to persuasion. Without the working of the Spirit on the heart, the hearer cannot be persuaded. Yet God does use human means to accomplish his work. The Bible exhorts the preacher to work hard (2 Tim. 2:15). By contrast, a claimed reliance on the Spirit may be an excuse for laziness. How many lives *haven't* been touched by the carefully chosen words of a preacher, be they warm words of encouragement or urgent words of warning!

Yes, better preaching wants to persuade. Paul sought this. The Bible describes his preaching by the word "persuasion." Yet a preacher's persuasion ought never be divorced from clear teaching. Such a failure gives a hollow sound to the sermon. The listener may be persuaded only of what he or she wants to hear. Or worse, people may be convinced of error if the sermon fails to build on the foundation of clear teaching.

What language persuades people? Evocative language that addresses the senses and taps the memory of experiences. When the Word of God is made real, when people can see exactly what we say and sense what we portray, then persuasion has been well used.

A persuasive style of preaching should be interesting and energizing. Emotional language need not be absent. The evocative element, however, looms large. Aspects such as descriptive language, vivid words, and sensory imagery mark evocative language. The persuasive style also employs analogy, example, and other figures of speech. The middle style of classical rhetoric stands close to a persuasive style of preaching. One way to visualize the persuasive style is like this:

	Clarity	Interest	Evocation	Energy	Emotion
P			******		
			******		
E			******		
			******		
R			******		
			******		
S			******		
			******		
U			******		
		******	******	******	
A		******	******	******	
	******	******	******	******	
D	******	******	******	******	
	******	******	******	******	
I	******	******	******	******	
	******	******	******	******	******
N	******	******	******	******	******
	******	******	******	******	******
G	******	******	******	******	******

THE MOVING STYLE

Better preaching also intends to move people to respond to the Word of God. When people believe, they give more than intellectual assent to God's truth. Faith demands commitment, and commitment demands a response—a response that goes beyond lip service to all the issues of life. That's why preachers of the Good News seek action and reaction. If faith without works is dead, they will urgently seek to move their listeners to a lively demonstration of faith. Therefore they wield language that moves people and adopt a style that lights the fires of response. Although the characteristics of a message that moves people include its content and organization, language plays a vital role in the process.

In the same way that hollow persuasion neglects the foundation of clear teaching, so it is a manipulative emotional device that is employed for its own sake. Urgently seeking commitment or action without clearly presenting foundational truths, and without persuading people of their validity and value, is as removed from God's grand purpose as a message dominated by remote abstractions and fuzzy statements.

Yet there is language that moves people. We find it in Scripture. We hear it in better preachers who dare call for a response. Language can show the emotion of the speaker, but a higher purpose touches the core of the listener. The moving style echoes the high style recognized by classical rhetoric. It can be portrayed like this:

	Clarity	Interest	Evocation	Energy	Emotion
M					******
					******
O					******
				******	******
V				******	******
			******	******	******
I			******	******	******
			******	******	******
N		******	******	******	******
	******	******	******	******	******
G	******	******	******	******	******

IMPLEMENTING THE THREE STYLES

The illustrations of the three styles are meant only to be suggestive. A case for a hard-and-fast relationship of the teaching, persuading, and moving styles to the elements of language ought not be made. If a flexibility of expression is maintained, an overlapping and mixing of styles will sometimes occur.

How can you put this information on a theory of style to work? I suggest an exposure to these principles over a period of time. An attempt to implement the concepts after three easy lessons will fail, and the results of a mechanical approach will become all too evident.

How can you absorb these principles? One way is by listening to and reading the sermons of others, noting how they make use of these concepts or fail to employ them. Listen to and read your own sermons with an eye to seeing how much you put these ideas to work.

Then practice. The pulpit, however, is not the best practice field. The pulpit should demonstrate the fruit of your attempts to implement these principles. Other teaching and speaking opportunities may provide a better exercise arena. The pastor's study serves as the best place to work on these suggestions until they get into the preacher's speech and become natural. Naturalness—that's a goal! Allow these principles to find their way into your speaking until you need give the matter only a little thought.

Be warned of side effects! The goal of our preaching cannot be the demonstration of a clever style. If a sermon is style conscious, it fails miserably. The preacher then stands like a carpenter with a gold-plated hammer without nails, wood, or blueprint for the house. "See how swiftly I swing my lovely hammer?" To use a different metaphor, style is like the little feather on the arrow's shaft. It belongs on the arrow and not in the preacher's hat. Incisive, effective language in preaching must always be a tool working for the benefit of the sermon; it is a simple but pivotal part to guide the message to the heart of those who hear.

Some preachers sink into stylistic ruts and develop only one element of a style. It's possible to preach clearly without preaching persuasively. Some preachers major in an interesting style. Still others move quickly to the emotional element. Two of the styles described in the introduction demonstrate these problems. Such preachers need to ask questions such as "What am I called to do with God's Word when I proclaim it to these people?" and "How can I purposefully apply principles of style to achieve that goal?"

The issues discussed in this chapter become clearer in part 3, "The Elements of a Preaching Style." These suggestions are made in the hope that careful, intelligent, and purposeful choices can be made so that preaching may be "clear," "full of grace," and "seasoned with salt" (Col. 4:4–6).

Part 3

The Elements of a
Preaching Style

8

Clarity

When a preacher effectively brings the thoughts of the sermon to the mind and heart of the listener, then clarity has been achieved. Clarity depends on cogent ideas presented in a logical manner. Style, however, makes its own contribution to clarity. It is possible to cloud a message having an essentially good structure through language that is not clear. If the preacher's purpose is to inform, then the sermon fails completely when it lacks a clear style. A sermon designed to persuade stumbles without the light of clarity. Aristotle said, "Speech which fails to convey a plain meaning will fail to do just what speech has to do."[1] Clearness, then, is the first order of business of a good style; it builds a foundation under all the other elements.

Several aspects of language help to clarify thought. Let's examine these aspects more closely.

THE RIGHT WORD

Precision is essential in many disciplines. Carpenters, engineers, and parachutists must all be exact in their work. This is true of preachers. It is imperative that their language be precise. There is no substitute for using the right word at the right time.

This idea sounds simple, but there are complications. Many of us choose words that only vaguely approach the thought. It is easy to get lazy. But sloppy word choice has mortally wounded many sermons. They suffer silent deaths.

Certain questions are helpful to ask ourselves concerning important words of the sermon. Is there any other word that could better represent my idea? Am I sure of the meaning of the word I've chosen? Once I have picked the right word for its precise meaning, am I certain my audience will understand it? Should I explain it or place the word in a context that avoids misunderstanding?

Fine-tuning word choice is vital. The Bible corroborates this. The words of Scripture are sometimes so crucially important that the full weight of a thought hangs on just one word. Jesus appealed to the iota and dot of the law (Matt. 5:18). He argued for the Resurrection on the basis of the tense of a verb (Matt. 22:32). Paul reasons from the fact that a word is singular and not plural (Gal. 3:16). Some preachers, by contrast, proclaim the Word by throwing handfuls of ambiguous terms at the congregation in the hope that something will hit the mark. Most of these words don't hit anything but the floor. Take this example:

> James says that people must be better listeners and shouldn't get so excited, or vehement, or so red in the face with rage.

A clearer way to express the thought of James 1:19 is,

> Listen carefully. Then, answer thoughtfully. That's how to restrain your rage.

Words are tools in the preacher's workshop. He who knows the names and uses of his tools makes the better craftsman. A word that expresses too little or too much or is too general will hinder communication. I recommend buying a good dictionary. The classic *Oxford English Dictionary* gives not only the meaning of a word, but a history of its use. If you don't mind peering through a magnifying lens at ultra-fine type, there is a microprint edition of this grand old work available in two volumes that won't break the budget. Set a contemporary dictionary beside this classic, however, for you want to address today's people with today's language.

C. S. Lewis tells us that words lose their content and change their meaning over a period of time.[2] Preachers do well to be aware of such changes. For instance, the word *sickening* formerly described the cause of vomiting. Now it's an ejaculatory term for the frustrated.

The history of a word often adds a dimension to its meaning. An anonymous fourteenth-century worker may have first spotted the resemblance between a builder's hoist and the neck of a feeding crane. Once the connection is made it's difficult not to see something of the bird in that piece of construction machinery. A Roman saw the rippling motion of muscle beneath the skin as *musculus* or a "little mouse." We who see raw power in the word ("he muscled his way in") gain perspective from the word's humble origin.

Theological words also have a history. The word *atonement* doesn't mean much to most people, although they're comfortable with it as a religious term. Its older sense helps capture lost meaning. Instead of saying,

His death made an atonement for sin,

the preacher can explain what the word originally meant and declare,

He died to make an onement with God.

Doesn't the rephrasing make the idea vivid? That's the point.

Sometimes even little words obscure the point the speaker wants to make. For example:

Bitterness stood between her and her husband and their children.

Her bitterness divided her from her husband and also stood between her and her children.

Use *between* with two objects and *among* with three or more. The second statement gains clarity because of a better use of "between."

Here's another instance where one word changes the entire point:

> Paul literally climbed the mountains to win the Gentiles for Christ.

What the speaker meant was,

> Paul climbed over mountains of opposition to win nations for Christ.

Clearly the person didn't know the difference between "literally" and "figuratively." Thoroughness makes a difference!

There are countless examples that show the value of careful word choice. When do you "imply" and when may you "infer"? When do you use "farther" and when is "further" in order? Is something a "fact" or an "opinion"? Do you have "evidence" or "proof"? Are you being "convinced" or "persuaded"? I am "obliged" to end this paragraph before you become bored, but I am not "obligated" to do so. Little words mean a lot.

Using the right word in the right way with a sharp sense of its meaning aids the sermon in two ways. It conveys the meaning of the preacher's thought accurately, and it prevents confusion over contrary messages. A careless style can crackle with distortion and convey a message contrary to the content of the sermon. Teaching the need for disciplined living with sloppy, careless, undisciplined language conveys a mixed message at best. At worst, the delivery gives a subliminal message that denies the content's importance.

Don't limit the study of words to a random look at the dictionary. There's another word book available—your environment. Listen to people speak, especially those of your church and community. You can soon discover many things about people by listening to what they say and how they say it. This will help you to use words more effectively.

SIMPLE WORDS

There is a tendency among the educated to choose the long, latinate, polysyllabic designation. The four or more years spent in the environment of an institution of higher education conditions the scholar to communicate with complicated words. Although functional in certain contexts, they are better suited to writing than to speaking.

The writer may get by with the fifty-dollar designation since a reader can vary the pace, stop to reflect, reread, and look up a word in the dictionary. But the listener doesn't have time for that. He gets only one chance. The word the speaker chooses had better communicate clearly or the message passes by the listener.

Take a look at a long word with several syllables. What is it made of? Consider the word *polysyllabic*. If we syllabify "polysyllabic," we discover several parts arranged in three compartments. The root comes from "syllable" (already compounded from two Greek words), meaning "a part of a word pronounced with a single sound." In addition to that rather abstract idea, the word conveys the idea of "many." The adjectival ending indicates that this is a quality. So in the three-compartment package we find "the quality of having many word parts." All that must be comprehended by the listener in a fraction of a second. When we pile up complex words in our sentences, we are asking people to quickly open these complicated packages, rapidly scan the varied contents, and hurry on to the next one. Fatigue sets in.

Why not use short words? It can be done. Put a short word in place of a long one. Long words may make the speech grow pale and at times stale. Long words may not sound right. They can hide, blur, and show sham. Short words ring true. They have a clear sound like a bell. They say what they mean and give punch to your speech. So add zip to what you say and zest when you preach. Do not fear to use short words to speak with force and, yes, to make things clear.[3]

One way to practice the use of simple words is by

talking to children. The little people won't let you get by with flaunting complex words. A wrinkle of the nose and a quick question interrupt any word they don't understand.

SIMPLE LANGUAGE

In addition to simple words, choose simple expressions and sentences. Although saying too little can be a problem, preachers often say too much, needlessly complicating communication. Redundancies can creep into speech, such as *"refer back* to this passage I just quoted." This is incorrect. Make it either "turn back to" or "refer to." The "re" in refer means "back." Unnecessary words only clutter speech. Instead of saying, "Because of the fact that he made . . . ," say, "Because he made. . . ." We can often make our speech more concise.

Consider these: "They were of the opinion that . . ." versus "They thought . . ."; "I venture to say to you, speak the truth . . ." versus "Tell the truth." Once you start looking for ways to be more succinct, the process becomes easier. One way to start is to write out a taped sermon the next day. Be careful—this will be revealing! But this winnowing will allow you to say more with greater clarity.

Simple sentences aid clarity. All the conjunctions and prepositions in compound, complex, and especially compound-complex sentences, although sometimes necessary, stand like crossroads on the path toward comprehension, and they unduly complicate the already challenging process of speaking. Simple, well-constructed sentences say what should be said and move the listener at a steady pace.

Preachers can overdo simplicity, however. As sentences can get too long and complicated, they can also be too short and fail to say enough. Some people speak in fragments; we can't get to the idea without asking some questions. The preacher may stumble into the problem of "Joe loves the church less than Jane." The listener wonders, Is this a comparison between Joe's and Jane's love for the church—"Joe loves the church less than Jane loves the church"—or a comparison of Joe's interests—the church and Jane? Relative pronouns are often used for brevity's sake. Do they clearly refer to one person, or could they refer to more than one? On small matters like these, large clouds of confusion can condense.

SPECIFIC LANGUAGE

Each pair of sentences that follow illustrates the value of specificity.

Now, it says in the Bible somewhere. . . .
Paul, in 1 Corinthians 14:8, says. . . .

She got into an automobile and drove off.
She sped away in a shiny, black Lincoln.

The man lived over there on the other street.
John, a widower, lived in the green ranch on Grant Street, the place with the large spruce trees in the front yard.

Do you feel the difference in impact? We can't convey specific ideas in a general way. Generalities are often spoken when an idea hasn't ripened in the mind of the preacher. Specifics help the message affect the listeners: tell of "murder" instead of "crime." Specifics also encourage the listeners to apply the message: "take your wife out to dinner" is more practical than "show love to your wife."

UNCONVENTIONAL WORDS

People like to be able to understand one another. A departing saleswoman, commenting on the screen door of the parsonage, said, "Your door is kind of 'whopper-jawed.'" That sent the pastor to his dictionary to find out what's so whopper-jawed about his door. Webster hadn't heard of the word. A specialized dictionary provided the answer.[4] The term supposedly comes from southern Ohio and means "crooked," as a table with one short leg. A few weeks later the word emerged in one of his sermons.

That's a quaint way of speaking, but "whopper-jawed" is not a word known to the general population. Clarity demands familiar words. If the listener will not understand a word you plan to use, then explain it. If I had not explained "whopper-jawed," you might not have known what was meant. An unconventional word, like a smudge on a clean window, obscures the light of understanding and simply draws attention to itself.

ABSTRACTIONS

What is an abstraction? A number without reference to anything else is an abstract number. Attaching a number to an object (one year, two ears, or three deer) makes it concrete. When we mention an idea without describing the relation it has to other matters, we lose people in a cloud of abstraction. That's also true with words. When we choose words that have little or no association with the world of sense and matter, we sound ethereal. Abstract ideas and words tend to have no perceived practical use, so they fail to satisfy.

S. I. Hayakawa devised an abstraction ladder based on "Bessie the cow."[5] The animal as we perceive her munches grass near the bottom of the ladder. On the first rung is "Bessie," the name given to this particular cow. Bessie, however, has characteristics in common with other cows. When we call her a "cow," we move up a rung and already leave something behind—her individuality. She is also "livestock" (rung three), a characteristic of other animals like pigs and sheep. She has value and so stands among the "agricultural assets" on the fourth step. Since farm assets are among the many kinds of tangibles in this world, Bessie can be described as wealth. At this high level up the ladder, however, the rich smell of the dairy barn seems far away. How many people will think of Bessie when they hear of "the wealth of Wisconsin"?

An abstraction assumes that the listener knows enough to be able to substitute a word or an image from a lower rung of the ladder. That may not be true. A common word like "love," unless firmly bolted to concrete deeds, may send a listener up the ladder thinking, "Ah love, that beautiful quality of feeling that moves within the soul." He's lost in a cloud. The preacher should help the listener climb down by setting abstract words firmly in the context of the concrete and the specific.

Love—God giving his only begotten.

Jesus laying down his life for sinners: that's love.

Love is forgiving those who wrong you, including your enemies.

JARGON

Jargon has a habit of creeping into speech. It happens without the person's awareness. The church buys the minister a computer. So he throws his pencil away and processes words by machine. As he explores a new world, the congregation notices a change in his choice of words. The bulletin is "formatted," committees "interface" with each other, reports become "output," and people are "preprogrammed." A metamorphosis has occurred.

Specialties grow their own languages. The "in" words supposedly demonstrate that we belong to the club. Ignorance of the code leaves a person out in the cold. Preachers are exposed to many specialties and can pick up their jargon. Medicalese can be acquired at the hospital. Legal terms may come from that deacon who works for a law firm. Getting the car fixed will add a few mechanical terms. ("His temper rose; he was about to blow a head gasket.") Bureaucratese surrounds us all.

Preachers are theologians, but they may also specialize in church growth, leadership, and counseling. The parade of new therapies contributes to the vocabulary of some:

What I heard her saying was that she lacked holistic wellness and desired greater self-actualization.

Translated, the sentence sounds like this:

> She said she wants to put off old habits and become the kind of person God wants her to be.

Remove from the sermon's vocabulary most of those specialty words that creep up on the tongue. If you must use them, briefly explain them. Technical terms build dividing walls. Good communication breaks down such barriers with clear language that brings God's Word to people.

9

Interest

A boring sermon has a short lifespan. No matter how good the content may be, no matter how faithful to the Scriptures the message is, if it fails to interest, it doesn't reach the listener's heart.

Interest is the antidote to boredom. When we build interest into a sermon, the listener's attention level rises. Sometimes the content itself is interesting enough to carry people along. The style, however, adds to or detracts from the level of interest. What aspects of language bring interest to the sermon?

HUMAN INTEREST

The simple principle at work here is that people like to hear about people. The best examples of the power of the gospel are the experiences of people who have been touched by it. Clear demonstrations of failure lie in the sinful and selfish deeds of people. The Scriptures tell the story of God's redeeming grace in people's lives. We thrill to the story of Ruth. We shudder at the account of Ananias and Sapphira.

Scientific studies show that people are more interested

in reading about other people than about anything else.[1] A person's story captures more interest than an idea. People are usually more interesting than slides, objects, and outlines. A congregation listens more attentively when we tell a person's story. So the language of an interesting sermon will usually contain personal references.

> Let me tell you of the endurance of an elderly woman who lived for sixteen years with a broken hip.

Have I caught your attention? I thought so.

IMAGERY

Jesus used imagery in a way that grabbed the heart before the head could reject the message. "You are the salt of the earth" (Matt. 5:13). Are people salt? Do they have a crystalline structure? Of course not. The point of comparison between the way salt works and the influence of Christ's followers leads to a descriptive use of this taste to expand understanding. The saliva glands may actually function for a moment in response to the image, it is that vivid. Christ also said, "A city on a hill cannot be hidden" (Matt. 5:14). This image ignites your mind. "I am the bread of life," Jesus declared dramatically after feeding hungry thousands with five barley cakes (John 6:35).

Paul uses a military metaphor when he writes of the whole armor of God (Eph. 6:10–17). He also portrays runners in the stadium (1 Cor. 9:24–27). He mentions the body (Eph. 1:22–23) and ligaments (Col. 2:19). He alludes to the sea (Eph. 4:14) and to the market (2 Cor. 5:5). There may even be a suggestion of the theater in 1 Corinthians 4:9.

The Psalms overflow with imagery. "He is like a tree planted by streams of water" (Ps. 1:3). "The words of the LORD are flawless, like silver refined in a furnace of clay" (Ps. 12:6).

Look to the prophets. They are full of word pictures. "My people . . . have forsaken me, the spring of living water, and have dug their own cisterns, broken cisterns that cannot hold water" (Jer. 2:13).[2]

One way to summarize Jeremiah's difficult calling is the following: The person who teaches unpopular ideas often faces isolation. A more interesting approach sounds like this: Unpopular truth shines like the lonely beam of a night watchman's light. Sharp images have a cutting edge.

Some biblical images fail to speak to a twentieth-century audience. "He drives like Jehu" demands an acquaintance with the life of the Israelite king and chariot driver. Classical images may also fail to stir the modern mind. "He won a pyrrhic victory" confuses the listener who doesn't know the details of the victory of the king of Epirus over the Romans. "He majored in himself" is fine for college students and graduates; what will some others see in their mind's eye, an army uniform? Images have to target the audience before they can make their mark.

CONTRAST

The jagged outline of dark pine branches frames the focus of the scene. The bright center of the photograph portrays a snow-dressed mountain. The picture on the office wall insists on your attention.

Preaching, likewise, is as much art as science. Although the content and structure of the sermon may show some contrast, language can also. Ancient orators delighted in the antithetical sentence; at times they enjoyed it too much. When judiciously employed, however, it adds to the level of interest in the sermon. The prophets as well as the Prophet made use of contrast. Listen to Isaiah: "Instead of the thornbush will grow the pine tree, and instead of briers the myrtle will grow" (Isa. 55:13). Jesus spoke to Simon the Pharisee: "You did not give me any water for my feet, but she wet my feet with her tears and wiped them with her hair. You did not give me a kiss, but this woman . . . has not stopped kissing my feet. You did not put oil on my head, but she has poured perfume on my feet" (Luke 7:44–46).

Antithesis still captures the attention of the audience:

He distributed abundant criticism, but closed his pocket
to the poor.

TENSION

Language that effectively builds tension keeps the listener coming back for more. Proverbs 2:1–5 does this nicely.

My son,
if you accept my words and store up
  my commands within you,
  turning your ear to wisdom
  and applying your heart to understanding,
  and if you call out for insight,
  and cry aloud for understanding,
  if you look for it as for silver
  and search for it as for hidden treasure,
then you will understand the fear of the LORD
  and find the knowledge of God.

The writer postpones the conclusion, keeping the reader in suspense wondering what the outcome will be. Such little details when well used make a sermon intriguing.

A series of questions also adds tension by postponing the answer.

Jesus compares himself to the bronze serpent Moses set on a pole. Do you look to Jesus? Do you see him as the Son of the living God? Does he draw you to himself? Has he freed you from the poison of evil? Has he healed you of your sin? Can you say today, "Oh, yes, I look to Jesus"?

Each question tightens the bowstring until the listener anticipates when it will finally fly. The thought climaxes with the answer.

INTERESTING EXPRESSIONS

Make use of a saying or create your own. Hone what you say into a memorable statement. Put it into a package small enough to carry home from worship. Jeremiah used a proverb that lives today: "The fathers have eaten sour grapes, and the children's teeth are set on edge" (31:29).

Think of the memorable statements Jesus uttered: "The Sabbath was made for man, not man for the Sabbath" (Mark 2:27). "Do not throw your pearls to pigs" (Matt. 7:6). "He must . . . take up his cross and follow me" (Mark 8:34). "But many who are first will be last, and the last first" (Mark 10:31). "Where there is a dead body, there the vultures will gather" (Luke 17:37).

A preacher described the security we have in God, a security greater than that provided by pension funds and life insurance. He made his point in an interesting, memorable way when he said, "You're in good hands with . . ." while holding his hands in a gesture familiar to all who had seen a well-known advertisement. He paused to let the name of an insurance company silently echo through the minds of the congregation, and then said, ". . . God."[3] This caught the listener by surprise, and it said more of the superior security in the Lord than five minutes' worth of explanation could. It's a statement to carry home. I've retained it for several years.

EXAMPLE

The use of example goes to the boundary of the purpose of this book, and others have written of it at length. This section merely touches the surface of the subject.

Examples add light to the sermon. They draw back the drapes and flood the room with illumination. Some examples enhance the element of clarity. A touching illustration adds the element of emotion. But effective illustrations always add interest to the message.

Illustrations often make use of the rhetorical device

called analogy. There is a relationship between creation and the message of redemption: lilies, weather, rocks, and rivers convey God's truth. The customs of society, from barn storage to banquets, may portray God's Word.

An example need not always be an extended story. Some preachers spend ten minutes on one example, even though a few sentences will often do. Short examples can be piled up for effectiveness. Sermons without illustrations often serve seven-course meals of mincemeat: heavy, hard to digest. By contrast, examples lighten and give life to a message.

QUESTIONS

Better preachers ask questions. Questions add tension to the sermon; they make people sit up and listen. For instance, the matter of the apostle Paul's influence could be addressed in this straightforward way:

> Paul was a powerful speaker. Some think he was a radical and that was the source of his power. Others say that he had magical power. Still others point to wisdom as the source of his power. He, however, possessed power because he was a reformer and possessed divine power.

Now listen to Chrysostom in a sermon entitled "In Praise of St. Paul."

> What then do you say? What is the source of his power? He was subversive perhaps? His precepts were not those of a subversive, and there were many such. He was a magician perhaps? That is not the impact of his doctrines. Besides, there has never been any scarcity of magicians. He was a wise man perhaps? Wise men have always been plentiful. What then was the source of his power? For no one even remotely approximated it. Obviously it was not because he was a magician, or a subversive, but because he was a reformer and possessed divine and invincible power.[4]

Chrysostom's questions create a dialogue with his congregation. He imagines their questions and objections and then answers them.

VARIETY

Monotony saps the life from a sermon. Predictability denies hearers the thrill of discovery. A preacher who always mentions "the cattle on a thousand hills" in his prayer becomes known by that phrase. He who says things the same way with the same style and the same words is inviting his hearers to sleep. His message becomes the lapping of the lake upon the shore: steady, regular, predictable.

If you want to repeat a word used in a previous sentence, strive to use a synonym instead. Repetition serves learning, but there are dozens of ways to make a statement. Wield the richness of the English language to advantage. All the words imported from various sources into America's native language provide no excuse for saying the same thing in the same way at the same time and place.

Instead of repeating "the Bible says" each time you quote Scripture, vary the announcement. You can say "the Scriptures inform," "the Word declares," "Matthew writes," or "Jesus promises."

Imagine that you want to tell of a woman who persisted in prayer. One way to say it is this:

> She prayed, and she prayed, and she prayed some more.

Using variety gives statement more interest:

> Oh, how she prayed! She appealed to her Lord. She begged him. She threw herself at his feet.

or

> She prayed to God. Her words honored him. How she blessed him! She lifted her praise to the heavens.

Vary the style. A persuasive part of the sermon

shouldn't have the same style as a section of instruction. Why should the preacher speak of the glorious truths of the gospel in a dry manner suited to teaching arithmetic? Or why preach with an unvaried shout and language suited for an emergency?

Vary sentence length, vary sentence structure, and avoid the predictable. The point is not to demonstrate cleverness but to bring God's message with vitality.

ARCHAIC LANGUAGE

"Dearly beloved, it behooves us today to speak of unfeigned charity." No, this is not from a yellowed love letter of a previous century. It's a sermon style present in the twentieth century! Some think religious matters need a special style. The words come from the nineteenth century or from older versions of the Bible. "Wrought," "even," "like unto," "beseech," "nigh," "hast," and similar words find their way into twentieth-century speech. Some preaching is studded with these old stones.

The archaic style tells the listener that biblical truths live in a musty monastery walled off from the everyday world. Archaisms say that the teachings of Scripture require an old stained-glass sanctuary and "religious" language. A preacher who delights in archaic language risks making his sermon a museum piece. Some, tutored with archaic language, think they cannot pray in public or talk of their faith because they haven't learned the language. That usually means they haven't mastered archaic language. There's no need for such speech. The language of preaching ought to be the language of the people enhanced by the message preached.

10

Evocation

Evoke [e-vōk']: to call (a feeling, faculty, manifestation, etc.) into being or activity. Also, to call up (a memory) from the past.[1]

Some styles leave ideas lying in the dust. Evocative language, however, brings thought to life and gives it a visible and tangible quality. It does that by appealing to the listener's memory of experiences. When speakers communicate a new idea in a manner that connects it to what a person already perceives, they foster understanding. Language may do that by painting a word picture. It may also make use of senses other than sight. When preachers receive the response, "Ah, now I see," they have tapped the persuasive power of evocative language. Evocative language includes many aspects. Let's take a look at them.

DESCRIPTIVE LANGUAGE

Preachers who practice the art of description will be able to portray God's truth in a vivid way. If they want to communicate essential truths found in 1 Kings 17, they might say,

> This chapter tells of Elijah's warning to King Ahab that
> God would judge the land with a drought that could not
> end except by the word of the Lord announced by the
> prophet. Elijah then exiled himself from the king and
> later from the land of Israel.

Such a statement expresses the chapter's concern
plainly enough, but it doesn't involve listeners in the drama
of the passage. Imaginative, descriptive language takes
listeners by the hand, transports them to the land of Israel at
about 845 B.C., and lets them see what happened.

> Watch him go. The cool ravine is now far behind. He
> travels through a landscape burnt brown by the sun.
> Drooping trees shimmer in the heat. Rustling locusts
> fight for the last blades of grass. The bawling of a
> starving calf sounds across the field. He pauses a
> moment at the boundary marker. Then Elijah moves on.
> He carries heavy baggage. The prophet travels bur-
> dened by knowledge that the land and its people will
> not see renewal until the Lord speaks again. And he,
> Elijah, the Lord's spokesman, forsakes Israel.

A verbal description is greatly improved by language
aimed at the senses. A slide or two could evidence a drought
but would lack the movement, the drama, the variety of
sights, sounds, and smells evoked by a verbal description.
Even a video-recording would lack elements of a good
description and remain two-dimensional. Time, distance,
depth, sound, and smell pose no problem for descriptive
language. That inner screen of mind and heart on which a
descriptive scene plays may have more sparkle than the pull-
down kind, especially if the listener has a little imagination.

Descriptive language stimulates the inner eye as well as
the other senses; it creates scenes within the mind of the
listener. To describe something, however, it's necessary to
see it first yourself. If you don't visualize what you want to
say, then the listener will have difficulty seeing it. When
carefully planned and properly executed, descriptive language delights the listener and assists persuasion. When a

preacher moves from dull statements to vivid portrayals, people will take life-changing ideas home from church.

Learn from the Bible. It offers not only precisely organized statements, but also stories, personal incidents, and national struggles. It portrays shepherds, vines, yokes, cups, rocks, roads, and rivers.

Be sensitive to God's creation. Spend some time outdoors. Look, listen, smell, touch, taste. Make a conscious effort to put your senses to work. See if you can stretch your sensitivity and expand your awareness of what's about you.

Be aware of people. How does a seventy-year-old grandmother differ from her seventeen-year-old granddaughter? Can you see the difference in your mind clearly enough to describe it?

Read descriptive language. A storyteller must master the art of description. How does a word painter sketch a muggy August day in Indiana? Maybe you can learn how to describe a hot day in Israel.

Listen to people speak, especially common folk who often talk descriptively. The meteorologist describing a downpour may tell of 4.9 inches of precipitation falling in 7 hours and 17 minutes; the church custodian calls all that rain "a real gully-washer." An elder described the anger and frustration of a fellow church member in these words: "He stamped his foot so hard his sock fell down." You may not want to imitate some of the descriptive language you hear about you, but you can learn from it.

ANALOGY

Although analogy sometimes describes relationships in general, its better use compares relationships. As light is to the eye, so knowledge is to the mind: these relationships are analogous.

Here's another illustration of the value of analogy. The younger generation frequently finds it hard to explain the intricacies of the computer to those raised with mechanical adding machines and muscle-building typewriters. So when a man asked his son why some of the computer equipment occasionally failed to react to commands, he was prepared for an answer in a "foreign tongue." What he got was an analogy: "The pieces of equipment are like people on a thick rug trying to shake hands. If you turn the switches off and on or in the wrong order, it can be like trying to shake hands with static electricity jumping between fingers." Dad, intimidated by the equipment and not at all literate in the language of the computer world, actually understood what his son meant. That's the point of an analogy.

Although the language of this example is quaint, the analogy still rings true.

> A mother hates the disease that is in her child; but does she abandon the child, saying, "I hate morbid conditions of every kind," and let the child die, as a testimony to her dislike of violations of natural law? Is it not a better testimony to her hatred of disease, that night and day she lingers over the little sufferer till she brings it back to good health? Is that not a better way of hating disease than the other would be? That is the true hatred of sin which kills it by kindness.[2]

It's difficult to comprehend ideas and relationships that have no reference to what you already know. But when a preacher makes use of analogy and builds on what a congregation knows, on life experiences and what they can easily imagine, then their world expands.

> Chicago's beautiful Buckingham Fountain sends a powerful stream hundreds of feet into the air. As evening's darkness settles on the city, ever-changing colors illumine gushing and tumbling waters. Pumps powered by mighty engines sing beneath the surrounding pavement building pressure great enough to raise that fountain high above the pool.
>
> A person's conviction powers the urge to speak of what he knows. If the engines of conviction sing, then the fountain will flow. If they sputter and die, then the lights will play upon a complacent pool.

IMAGERY

Imagery's territory is several acres larger than that of analogy, although the land overlaps. The speaker first creates a useful image in his own mind. He then conveys it in vivid language. If he succeeds, his language evokes a similar image in the mind of the listener, who then can take the thought home. Imagery helps to visualize the message. It strikes inner senses and taps a variety of experiences. Such preaching appeals to more than an inner sense of sight. Imagery has been defined as "words and phrases denoting a sense-perceptible object used to designate not that object but some other object of thought belonging to a different order or category of being."[3]

Like analogy, imagery is possible because the objects of this world and the customs of society may have more than one point of significance. They have their own significance, but they may also portray something other than themselves. Instead of saying that kings will always be among Judah's descendants, Jacob's deathbed prophecy announces, "The scepter will not depart from Judah" (Gen. 49:10). The scepter is not a line of kings, but the picture of a scepter handed down over generations portrays lineage. Balaam, the reluctant preacher, said, "A star will come out of Jacob" (Num. 24:17). A star is a distant sun seen on a clear night. The promised Son, like the star, rises, shines, and gives light in darkness. Calling the Son of Promise a star visualizes him for us. It creates a picture, possibly a moving picture, in the mind.

Paul writes imaginatively when he says, "If any man builds on this foundation using gold, silver, costly stones, wood, hay or straw, his work will be shown for what it is" (1 Cor. 3:12–13). "But we have this treasure in jars of clay to show that this all-surpassing power is from God and not from us" (2 Cor. 4:7).

An image often lies behind metaphysical and theological words. "Goodness" seems a lofty, vague ideal. Wipe away the dust of the ages and you find "God." Goodness is

Godness. Polish the word "truth" and you will see a bride and groom "plighting their troth." "Adoption" frames a picture of a father gathering a little urchin in his arms. "Sanctification" hides a saint.

Words that describe emotions, sentiments, qualities, and other abstract entities often have roots that speak of real, physical, sensible objects. To bring a designation to earth, it may be necessary to recall the root word. "Designation," an etymological dictionary tells you, hides the image of a scribe making marks on stone. Words that carry weight across the bridge of communication wear the clothes of matter and sense.

Preachers can learn from their Lord. Jesus had the eye of a poet for imagery. He used image upon image, not to embroider the truth, but to reveal God's Word plainly. The Sermon of the Mount abounds with such pictures.

> Why do you look at the speck of sawdust that is in your brother's eye? (Matt. 7:3).
>
> Enter through the narrow gate (Matt. 7:13).
>
> Watch out for false prophets. They come to you in sheep's clothing (Matt. 7:15).
>
> Everyone who hears these words of mine and puts them into practice is like a wise man who built his house on the rock (Matt. 7:24).

Is imagery among the reasons why the crowds were astonished at the teaching of Jesus and why his teaching struck so deeply when compared with the pedantic instruction of the scribes?

Some preachers harness the strength of imagery and use it for important purposes. Even difficult and controversial concepts can be apprehended through imagery. Listen to a preacher weave a fictitious scene around the image of a star:

> Every now and then, we hear a rumor that some of God's own children have fallen from grace; I do not believe it. It is said that they have fallen away and

perished; I do not believe it. Those of you who go out
late at night, may see a great many shooting stars; and
some of your little children will cry, "Look, father, the
stars are falling"; and possibly some children will
believe that stars have fallen from their places. Take the
telescope and look at the heavens; sweep the sky as far
as the range of the instrument will permit. Jupiter is all
right, and Saturn, and Mars, and Venus, and Mercury,
and all the planets, they are all in their places; and the
fixed stars are shining on as they have done ever since
the Lord first kindled them to charm away the gloom of
night. I do not know what these shooting stars may be
. . . neither do I know what these apostates may be,
there have been a great many guesses about these that
did flame out so brightly once. But I do know this, that
Jesus still holds the seven stars in his right hand, and he
will not drop even one of them; they shall not be
reduced to six, or five, or four, or three, or two, or one,
or vanish altogether; neither shall it ever be so with any
of the true sons of God.[4]

This is an excerpt from Charles Haddon Spurgeon's preaching on Revelation 1:16, a passage itself heavy with symbolism. He builds on symbol in a remarkable way. He uses analogy and metaphor. He impresses the image of flaming stars on our minds. He contrasts them with the permanent bodies. We can watch the telescope sweep the sky. We sense the gloom of darkness. He denies that we will ever see the stars dribbling through the Lord's fingers, a picture with progression. All this comes in a passage that is brief, but remarkably rich. He makes us see what he says. That's the function of imagery.

Often a short image will suffice. When commenting on John 8:56 we may be tempted to say that Abraham's experiences with God allowed him to visualize the fulfillment of promise. That's true enough. But if people will see the truth, we will want to state it something like this:

> As Abraham climbed the mountain of faith, he stopped, and looked to the distant horizon. What a view! Look how far he could see! He could see all the way to Jesus.

Imagery can not only impress a biblical message on the listener, but also portray a real-life situation.

> The world we live in is like a house floating off its foundation. Open the cellar door. Look down. There's nothing there.

It's important that images lie within the world of experience of those addressed. They must come from plants, animals, products, occupations, and practices of the times and place of the listeners. It won't do to picture an item of sailing equipment to a prairie-bound landlubber, unless it can be quickly and graphically explained.

It's also necessary to understand how biblical images may differ from our own experience. "God is our rock." Most see a large, solid boulder when they hear "rock," but the Israelite saw a fortress. Also, a long acquaintance with the Scriptures makes biblical imagery familiar to the preacher, but the audience may not be as well acquainted with such pictures.[5]

SENSE APPEAL

Sight is not the only sense the preacher can address. People also hear, smell, taste, and touch (including inner feelings and a sense of movement). Evocative language can reach any sense through the ear.

The Scriptures abound with an appeal to the senses. Allegorical writers such as John Bunyan made use of biblical description and added to it from the stock of their own imagination. Spurgeon, more than any other preacher, excelled in appealing to all the senses.[6]

Preachers who want to emphasize a thought or image ask how they can help the people not only see it, but also hear it, feel it, taste it, and smell it. They will place earphones on people so they hear buzz, crackle, and rattle with the inner ear. They will invent "smellevision" and make the inner nostrils twitch. They will help the audience savor goodness or taste bitterness. People will feel the wind; they will soar and plunge through the preacher's language.

Sense appeal not only portrays the Savior by way of sight, but lets people hear the sound of his sweet call. It not only paints a picture of the goodness of the Lord, but helps people taste it. The sweet, clean air of heaven will be in their nostrils; the stink of sin as well. They will feel the guiding hand of the Lord on their arm or the heavy burden of judgment on their back.

Evocative language tries coming in from the east and then the west, and if necessary, will helicopter down from above or tunnel up from the bottom. This kind of language drives thought through more than one gate to get the message home. It delivers the goods right into the house and on the kitchen table rather than leaving a cold package on the doorstep.

The preacher who is sensitive to the senses can let the congregation hear trumpets sound with joy and cymbals crash with vanity. They will feel Jacob's deceptive cloak as surely as Isaac's gnarled fingers. They will taste the Word that is sweeter than honey. They will smell the pure offering of prayer. People will hear heavy timbers scrape over the cobbles of Jerusalem's streets. They will hear the hammer pound nails and feel the cross thud into the socket with a flesh-tearing jolt as soldiers raise Jesus above the earth. The rumble and scrape of the stone rolled away on resurrection day will sound in their minds. The winds of Pentecost will blow again and their sound heard. The preacher is limited only by biblical truth, by his own imagination, and by a sense of what is appropriate. People raised in the video age are open to sensory language.

How would you describe Jonah's sudden disembark-ment assisted by the sailors? "The sailors threw Jonah overboard. Splash!" To impress the act upon the listener, mine the resources of sense appeal. You could try this instead:

What was it like aboard that boat? The mountainous seas crash upon the little ship and its men. The wind in the rigging rises to a high-pitched scream at the crest of every wave. The water peels off the surface of the sea. It stings the eyes of the sailors; it beats like stones upon their backs. The sailors struggle to lift the cursed prophet, and they fling him over the rail. You hear no splash above the roar. The surging sea separates him from the ship, and the waters close over Jonah. Then the whistling wind lowers its pitch. The sea no longer crashes. Blue sky chases the dark clouds away. Now the crew stands in awed silence on the tangled deck sucking in the delightful smell of a clean, fresh breeze that follows the storm. Meanwhile. . . .

How would you impress the truth of justification by faith on people? Why not bring them into the courtroom? Let them see the Judge robed in majesty. Make them smell the rot recorded in dank books that spell out every crime. Help people hear projectors whir and tape recorders whine out evidence of a life of law-breaking. Let sinners wait in dry-mouthed silence for the solemn verdict. Then turn their eyes to the Advocate, the Lawyer with scars on his forehead and holes in his hands. Force the question upon them: "Do you believe?" Let them feel his loving arm around them as a new verdict—"No condemnation"—echoes through the courtroom.

Abstract preaching limited to rational categories appeals to a person as a reasoning machine. People stand taller than that. Limiting description and imagery to the visual sense underestimates the ability of people. They are more than mind and eyeballs. Imagery that appeals to the various senses addresses the whole person.

If unknown ideas and even abstract thoughts can be communicated by calling up known, remembered experiences, then why not employ all the variety of experiences people have had? Throw open the whole warehouse of their experience. There's no reason for the preacher to leave the doors of sense perception locked or to limit his entry to the visual room of this vast storehouse. It's not easy work. But the preacher who develops a sensitivity to the world around him, who has imaginative ability, and who can describe what he senses will find a reward in sermons that reach the heart.

DIRECT ADDRESS

Direct address is a little tool that brings immediacy to a sermon. Instead of describing what people say, let them say it for themselves. Rather than talking about what Isaiah said to the people of his day, we can bring biblical figures into the pulpit and let them speak.

We can report on what Peter penned this way:

> Peter, in 1 Peter 3:8, writes that we ought to live in harmony with each other and have sympathy, love, compassion and humility as well.

Or, let him speak for himself:

> Peter has this to say. "Live in harmony with one another, be sympathetic, love as brothers, be compassionate and humble."

> Did you know that Isaiah preached a Good Friday message? Would you like to hear what he said? You can still hear him preach today. Listen! "Surely he took up our infirmities and carried our sorrows, yet we considered him stricken by God, smitten by him and afflicted. But he was pierced for our transgressions, he was crushed for our iniquities . . . " (Isa. 53:4–5).

This practice brings the listener one step closer to the action. When we get rid of those "thats" which introduce sections describing what was said, we bring a sense of immediacy to the speech. It's like the difference between watching the event take place and reading about it later in the papers.

Some of the most picturesque passages of Scripture contain dialogue. Read the first two chapters of Ruth with an eye for direct address and especially dialogue. Consider the striking conversation between Satan and God in the opening chapter of Job.

The preacher can also create a dialogue within the sermon, permitting the congregation to listen in, let's say, on an imaginary counseling session.

"Well, John, tell me in plain words what you think the problem is."

"It's my wife, pastor. I just can't stand her anymore."

"You can't stand her? But God wants you to love her. He commands that in his Word. Here, I'll show you."

"Yes, I know all about that. But you don't know my wife. We just don't get along anymore."

"You mean to tell me that you and your wife are no closer than, say, a neighbor?"

"Yeah, that's it. We're that far apart."

"But the Bible says you are to love your neighbor. Here. . . ."

"Sure, I know what you mean. But she nags and argues and fights all the time. I don't think God wants people to fight like we do. I just don't want to live that way any more. I'm ready to call it quits."

"You mean there's war in your house! You must be like enemies."

"Yes, I suppose it is that bad. We do fight like enemies."

"John, God says to love your enemies. Remember how Jesus forgave those who nailed him to the cross? He wants you to forgive your wife. There's no escape from that. You can learn to forgive her. You can also learn to love her since you, John, know that God loves you."

RHETORICAL FIGURES

Today's rhetoric divides the figures of speech into schemes and tropes. Schemes are the structural changes in words and sentences that enhance the style. Alliteration, antithesis, chiasm, and parallelism stand among the schemes. The tropes have to do with meaning. Allegory, hyperbole, metaphor, rhetorical question, and simile can be included among the tropes.

A few modern preachers could use Quintilian's ancient advice: "With regard to genuine figures, I would briefly add that, while suitably placed they are a real ornament to style, they become perfectly fatuous when sought after over-much."[7] Since they are fun to use, figures can be over-worked and can merely call attention to themselves. They may also direct the attention to the preacher. Consider the following sample:

> So Paul rightly concludes that he can stand before God's throne without a gram of fear; that in everything, in all cases, under all circumstances, he can make known to his Lord the requests of his aching heart; that he can be absolutely sure that God, hearing his requests, will roll up His celestial sleeves and do something about those pleas; that he can therefore pull up the windows of his mind and toss out all that is worrying him; that he can push open the doors of his heart and sweep out all that is hurting him . . . ; that he can lift the lid on his music box . . . ; that he can encourage his . . . congregation members to follow in his foot-steps, laying before God their prayer books.[8]

Dessert's a tasty morsel that delights the senses, but too much of it brings on a reaction. The section quoted is too rich. In one extended sentence we are taken from heaven to earth, from the bedroom window to the back door, on to the parlor, and then the prayer chamber, with brooms, music, and footpaths somehow mixed in. It leaves the impression of busy-ness and nervous movement.

The best that can be said for this preacher is that he isn't afraid of using figures of speech. Although figures can be overused, misused, or used in a self-serving way, most preachers, it seems, fail to tap their potential. Figures serve a good purpose. *Metaphors* and *similes* in particular make ideas approachable. A simile is a simple comparison introduced by the words "like" or "as," as in "It is like precious oil poured on the head" (Ps. 133:2). "The LORD is your shade" (Ps. 121:5) uses metaphor. The warning against mixing metaphors may be the only advice about figures some have heard.

Other figures that pluck the strings of imagination include *personification*, as in "Lift up your heads, O you gates" (Ps. 24:7). The sound-effect words (such as the laughter in Isaac's name) are usually called *onomatopoeia*. The word "gram," in the excerpt given above, is an example of *metonomy*—the naming of one thing to represent another closely associated object. Figures of speech, however, must remain servants of the Word, not spotlights on the preacher. When used with wisdom they give a perceptible dimension to the message.

CLICHÉS

I learned how easy it is to pick up a cliché. My wife and I visited an elderly man of the congregation. He prefaced many of his sentences with, "When it's all said and done. . . ." We discussed his habit on the way home. The following Sunday, to my utter amazement, I walked the beaten path of that old cliché in the sermon. To add insult to injury, when my wife heard what I said, she could scarcely contain her laughter. Out of the corner of my eye I saw her shoulders shaking. It came at the wrong psychological moment, the rug was pulled from under me, and I had to call a halt to the sermon. My wits were conspicuous by their absence, but rather than be caught between a rock and a hard place, between the cliff and the deep blue sea, I had to somehow get on with it or be a bump on a log. So be mindful of the fact that clichés abound, and when it's all said and done the odds are overwhelming that you will find a few in your speech as I have in mine.

A cliché, like an old rug, has lost its appeal because of wear. It no longer speaks. It fails to project an image in the mind of the listener. People no longer see "a rock and a hard place" with somebody caught, somehow, between the two.

He who creates fresh images adds sparkle and life to his thought. Get rid of that old rug! Avoid clichés.

Like clichés, some religious expressions are so over-worked that they no longer carry freight. It's true that we are to "give God the glory," but that phrase says very little to most people. Do you see the act of transferring the great weight of glory to God? There must be a "personal relation-ship with Jesus Christ," but Unitarians and the cults also use the phrase, so what does it say?

How about this one: "Everyone's a witness." Do you still see a witness stand? "The church is the family of God." Do you envision a family with father, mother, brothers, and sisters? These and many other phrases need fresh images. Some can be rescued when stated in a new way that allows the congregation to see it. If the sermon describes God's family in a tangible way, the listener may conclude that the church is the family of God without the preacher mentioning the phrase. A cliché tells the congregation that the speaker has no interest and no enthusiasm for traveling any other route than the well-worn rut.

11

Energy

Listening to an energetic speaker teaches something about style. What aspects of this person's style add energy to speech? Casual preaching strolls through the park on a balmy afternoon. Energetic speech bustles like a central city marketplace. Something exciting and important happens here, it seems to say. It is possible, of course, to have great energy without the content to match it. Some people get excited about small matters. At other times energy covers a lack of thought. An energetic speech with limited content is a lot of smoke, but shows no fire. I suspect, however, that the bigger problem in today's preaching is that great themes are expressed in a bland style.

A thoughtful, wise use of the following aspects of language brings vitality to the message, creating a lively and even powerful kind of preaching. What are these ingredients of language that add energy to a sermon?

VIVID WORDS

Vivid words are not found in specialized language that excludes an outsider. The unique words of a discipline do not make for vivid speech. Specialized language lacking lively words sounds like this:

> We all know that the fideistic stance is comprised of knowledge and assent.

> The command to sacrifice Isaac teleologically suspended the ethical question.

> The sagacious prophet's eschatological viewpoint fore-shortens the beyond.

The technical subject matter overwhelms style in these examples. Yet statements like these show up in sermons. The weak words completely short-circuit the power of thought for all except the initiated.

Ideas can show force and energy. Words can also sparkle and show vitality. It's possible to express powerful ideas in bland language totally unimpressive to the listener. "Take it or leave it," the style seems to say. But another speaker expresses his thought with more vigorous words that underscore the importance of the message. The examples mentioned can be stated more vividly:

> God wants you to understand his promise. He also wants you to trust, to lean on him and his promise. If you do understand his message and do trust his promise, you, my friend, have faith.

> God had his eye on the greater sacrifice of the Cross when he ordered Isaac to the altar. That's why he commanded what seems an intent to murder.

> As the prophet scans the future, he views Christ's first coming as at the same moment as the awesome hour of final judgment.

Look to the Bible for vivid language. Haggai doesn't have a reputation as a stylist, but he communicates energetically in the following example:

> "Give careful thought to your ways. You have planted much, but have harvested little. You eat, but never have enough. You drink, but never have your fill. You put on

clothes, but are not warm. You earn wages only to put them in a purse with holes in it. . . .

"You expected much, but see, it turned out to be little. What you brought home, I blew away. Why?" declares the LORD Almighty. "Because of my house, which remains a ruin, while each of you is busy with his own house" (Hag. 1:5–6, 9).

Haggai can be read without excitement, but the lively words and the simple yet strong style give a robust character to the message.

Luther stands high on the list of energetic preachers. Listen to him on John 3:16:

These are astounding words. God has every reason to be angry and to wipe out the world as a frightful enemy, and yet there is no greater lover than God, and no more desperate scoundrel than the world. To love the world and wish it well is beyond me. If I were God I would give it hell of fire. But instead of consuming the world in anger, God loves the world with such un-speakable and overflowing love that He gave His Son. My powers are not adequate to reach the bottom of this tremendous affirmation. This love is greater than the fire seen by Moses [in the burning bush], greater even than the fire of hell. Who will despair if God so loves the world?

The words read so simply but are so mighty. They are greater than the heavens and the sun. God will give us eternal life. If he offered us a dukedom or a kingdom, we should dispute and say, "It cannot be. He would not give me a kingdom." We think we are not worth more than twenty gulden, for what is man compared with God? But see now what God has in mind, that he should not strangle, terrify, and harass mankind, but rather should give life, and even eternal life.[1]

Luther didn't say, "Judge the world for its wickedness"; he said, "Wipe out the world as a frightful enemy." His way brings the thought to life and lets the hearer see God's hand at work. "God is merciful," it is true, but Luther's vivid expression is, "There is no greater lover than God." Instead of musing on inferiority, he says, "We think we are not worth more than twenty gulden."

The preacher can speak in a lackluster fashion, or he can imitate prophets and preachers whose speech brings life and energy to the subject.

ANGLO-SAXON WORDS

> I like the Anglo-Saxon speech
> With its direct revealings.
> It takes a hold and seems to reach
> Way down into your feelings.[2]

The English language has a history. It didn't drop upon the world fully developed. Its roots lie in the West-Germanic tribes that populated what is now Denmark. One tribe stands out. They lived near the sharp bend in the coastline and so were known as Angles. As Roman power declined in Britain, the Angles migrated across the channel. Eventually their language displaced the Celtic tongues across much of the island.

Other languages left their mark. Danish Vikings made a contribution to English. The Latin left behind by Roman conquerors was supplemented by the language of the church at an early stage and again by the scholar's tongue during the Middle Ages. The Norman invasion brought French, which became such a fad that it almost swept English aside. More recent centuries imported words from far and near.

Yet none can beat those early English words for zest. That's where we find some of the most vivid words in the language. Take advantage of Old English words: *land, hill, fight, light, sight, fear, dead, love, depth, dawn, hail, father, daughter, child, son, heaven, hell, buy, sell, will, guilt, forgive, worship.* Choose that short, snappy Anglo word, rather than the long, lazy Latin or frilly French version that has the same meaning. The native words contain power. Words derived from Latin and French tend to be coldly scientific or overly ceremonial. They are words of the treatise and the ornaments that embellish thought. "The Old West-Germanic words are the flesh and blood, bone and guts, hair and hide of the English language."[3]

The lazy Latin sentence sounds like this:

> Do not neglect the opportunity to purchase vintage and dairy products without any expenditure.

A short, snappy Anglo version sounds like this:

> "Come, buy wine and milk without money and without cost" (Isa. 55:1).

Don't announce it this way:

> Allow liturgical celebration to elevate you to celestial exaltation.

Rather, say:

> Let worship lift you to the heights of heaven.

SIMPLICITY

Energetic speech chooses simple structures and, especially, simple words. Don't say "abandon"; say "give up." Don't say "I appreciate your beneficial assistance"; make it "thanks for the good work." Forget "criterion"; say "standard," or better yet, "yardstick." Replace "Eliminate detrimental symbols" with "Get rid of dead words."

Remove the empty words from your speech. Routinely using words like *case, fact, nature, character, matter,* and *thing* indicates a habit of using empty words. Watch weighty relative pronouns such as "which." Drop it or change it to "that" when you can. Instead of saying "Paul, who was appointed an apostle, said," make it "The apostle Paul says." Compare these sentences:

> She is a woman with a generous nature.
> She's a generous woman.

Avoid qualifications unless they serve a purpose. Instead of stating,

> Love usually, with the exception of suspicious people and those who themselves are perpetual liars, believes what others say,

say,

> Love believes all things.

Attention to these little details will add energy to speech. Those who tell of the great things of God can place in his service that simple kind of speech that brings life and power to his message.

THE SECOND PERSON

Which statement mounts the platform?

> 1. It is best when the speaker makes use of the second person pronouns.
> 2. You had best use "you."

That "you" grabs the hearer in the second sentence as it measurably shortens the distance from speaker to listener.

Some preachers can't bear to use "you" except in words of praise. They express thoughts of duty, for example, with a first person plural—"we." It may be false humility that keeps the preacher from a straightforward "you." Being too nice can be added to the list of pastoral sins right after a lack of boldness. The prophets and the apostles didn't shrink from a good, hearty "you." They used it in words of encouragement, and they said "you" in warnings of judgment. Did Nathan say, "David, I know that we all have done things like that at one time or another?"

No, he said, "You are the man" (2 Sam. 12:7).

In like manner, don't say, "We all need faith and repentance in order to be saved." Do say, "God tells you, Repent and believe and you will be saved."

Better preachers throughout history have made good

use of the second person. So don't you take the detour through the back alley and sneak up to the back door of the house. Walk right up to the front door and knock.

One reason why some find it difficult to use the word "you" is the preacher's stance.[4] There is a "lecture stance" and a "preaching stance." The lecture stance describes the subject for people. It sounds like this: "Sanctification is a necessary ingredient of our salvation." The preaching stance declares the Word to the people. It sounds like this: "If you really believe it, your life will show it." Such preaching leaves the lecture hall and measurably shortens the distance between preacher and listener.

ACTIVE VERBS

Verbs come in two basic styles. Some verbs run, jump, play, and shout. Others just sit there. Some join the team and others are content to be spectators. The preacher's use of words may betray his mind-set. If he uses spectator verbs, he tends to portray a view of God's kingdom as static. If he uses active, marching, running, fighting verbs, he conveys the dynamite of the Word.

What are active verbs? All those that describe activity or movement. Verbs that do something are the active ones. Inactive verbs are, or are combined with, state-of-being verbs. Change intransitive to transitive, passive to active, and you will see sentences get off the benches and go to work. Get rid of some "is" verbs and their relatives such as "was," "will be," and the "been" constructions. In their place put living, running words that have far more energy than the fat, lazy ones asleep on the sidelines. Compare these two sentences:

> The Word of God is dynamite that is disintegrating old, sinful thought patterns and is a sword that is cutting away old habits.

> The Word of God dynamites old, sinful thought patterns and, like a sword, slices away old habits.

Yes, you may use "is" when needed. The Bible uses it with the greatest of subjects: "God *is* love." Truth not only moves and marches, but, thank the Lord, his truth abides. Yes, there is an "is-ness" about God's truth. Those who overemphasize the dynamic to the exclusion of a "thereness" of revealed truth also miss the point.

The question to ask, as with all these little issues of language, is "why?" Why should I use an "is" verb that tends to sit there? Would a marching verb be better? What do I intend to do? Perhaps you wish to convey a dependable characteristic of God. Then say it: "God is true to his Word." But if you wish to tell of the warm reach of God's mercy, then say, "The Father loves you." It's helpful to note that the ratio of active to passive verbs in the Bible is twenty active to seven passive.[5]

PRESENT TENSE

Don't always speak in the present tense, but do it as much as possible without putting a wrinkle into time. Should you say, "God in his Word, said . . . ," or "God says to you today . . ."? Did Paul say it long ago, or does he still speak?

> Paul, at about 60 A.D., wrote to the Philippians and said, "Do nothing out of selfish ambition or vain conceit, but in humility consider others better than yourselves."

> The Lord, through his apostle, says to you today, "Do nothing out of selfish ambition. . . ."

The preacher's set of mind determines how he expresses himself. If he shows remnants of Ramian-inspired Puritan methods, he will use the Scriptures as a theological resource book. His preaching will major in explanation, and then at some point the preacher will make the grand leap over the centuries to apply what he has learned from the ancient Scriptures to the present time. "What meaning does all that we have learned have for us today?" he will ask. Or, if the preacher overemphasizes the cultural background of the Bible, his sermon will conduct an "archaeological dig" into the past. Such preaching must work hard to overcome the weight of the past and make a good transition to the present. The history of preaching shows that even into this century, preachers in some quarters of the church clearly divided their sermons between teaching and application. A hymn sometimes marked the transition. Remnants of that practice remain.

Verb tense is also a subtle, but significant factor. God speaks today through revelation. God speaks most clearly today through the Scriptures. Since that's true, the preacher can speak in the present tense when he proclaims God's Word to people today.

SHORTER SENTENCES

Read the next two paragraphs out loud.

Rudolf Flesch proposes a sentence length difficulty scale that ranges from a very easy eight-word sentence to a very difficult sentence of twenty-four or more words, and that marks the line between short and long at seventeen words, which means that longer sentences should be broken into two parts—which advice should not be taken lightly.

Rudolf Flesch proposes a sentence length difficulty scale. It ranges from an easy eight-word sentence to a difficult twenty-four or more. The line between short and long falls at seventeen words. He suggests breaking longer sentences into two parts. That's usually good advice. Check your sentences.[6]

Although the subject matter of the paragraphs doesn't demand an energetic statement, the style of the second shows more force than the first one. Why? Shorter sentences.

12

Emotion

Preachers cannot avoid emotion. Their language always prods people to respond with some kind of feeling. "What type of emotion?" is the question to ask. Cool, even-tempered, abstract language may provoke some kind of emotional response. A low-key sermon on the mighty event of the Resurrection may elicit cold detachment or even irritation and impatience. An unrelieved stream of impassioned language may not always be the best means of gaining a response. Some preachers shed tears on the pulpit. Although circumstances may move a person to display emotion, the goal can be better served by thoughtful language designed to stir feelings.

Can the aspects of language that touch the emotions be defined? Frankly it's difficult to list them. The human feeling level is complex, people differ in their emotional responses, and feelings are too fleeting to be measured with a meter. Although we cannot chart its path, emotion does course through the heart and life of a person. Although emotional makeups differ, people do show a unity of response. And yes, it is difficult to spell out precisely how language effects the emotions. Nevertheless, it has an effect.

A list of the aspects of language that serve to touch the emotions overlaps some of what has already been been discussed. That's true of many of the aspects and all of the elements. If, for example, analogy serves the evocative element of language, that does not mean that it cannot also assist clarity and interest. Some aspects of evocative language rub elbows with the emotional element. Energetic speech and emotional language sometimes share the same house. Employing previously discussed aspects of language with the added layer of repetition often coaxes the emotional quality.

An examination of emotion-producing language helps to understand what it's like. Romans 8:28–39 shows some of the aspects of language that move people. Paul makes use of progression in verses 29 and 30. Take note of the series of questions beginning with verse 31. Look how he heaps up the possibilities in verse 35. Beginning with verse 38 he presents a series of contrasts. The contrasts lack precision, for he puts "powers" in the middle without any counterpart. He breaks off this string with an "anything else." The loose style conveys a sense of urgency like a traveler with little time to pack. All these features indicate the emotional element found in this section.

First Corinthians 6:2–10 also displays emotional aspects of language. Clusters of questions alternate with commands and exclamations. Look at the list that begins in verse 9. That's not an itemized shopping list. Paul isn't counting categories. Instead he is banging his fist. The drum beats emphasize the awful conclusion that such will not inherit the kingdom.

We hear that repetitive sound again in 2 Corinthians 6:2–10. How difficult it is to read the last part of verse 2 in a calm, matter-of-fact tone! "I tell you, now is the time of God's favor, now is the day of salvation." The rest of the section shows another compilation with a visceral, almost musical rhythm designed to impress the thought firmly into the listener. Halfway through, Paul adds contrast to the layers of impressions.

When you hear impassioned speech with words that inflame, take it as an opportunity to analyze. What gives this speech its emotional element? Listen to preachers who present an emotional style. Read conclusions to printed sermons, for you will most likely find the emotional element there, if it's present. The language of emotion, more than the other elements, is better caught than taught. Nevertheless, some aspects of this element can be listed.

DESCRIPTION

The aspect of description serves other causes.[1] But descriptive language plays a role in emotional language as well. A stirring moment described with feeling moves people. A touching moment described in an affecting way tugs at the heart. A moment of triumph or an occasion of sadness, when well described, affects the listener. Think of the description of the awesome Day of the Lord in 1 Thessalonians 4:16–17, or the powerful description of worship in Hebrews 12:18–24.

If you aim for greater faithfulness in reading the Bible and in attending corporate worship, you could choose a descriptive example to help people achieve these goals. Imagine that you know a retarded man:

> Let me tell you about Jimmy. Jimmy is a little slower than some. He never learned to drive a car. He travels the mile and a half to church on his bicycle, his Bible in the basket blowing in the wind. He comes to church alone. He knows no father. His mother works every day to support herself and her son. He's there every Sunday, rain or shine, in heat of summer and winter snow. Jimmy can't read much, though he's pretty good with numbers. When he hears his pastor announce the Scripture passage, his face wrinkles with concentration as he digs into his rumpled, rain-stained Bible, his index finger tracing Matthew or Hebrews or whatever the reading may be. He can't read well enough to keep up. But look how he struggles to find those chapters!

Jimmy has a ministry in his congregation. When people get lazy about worship, they often think of Jimmy. That sends them to church. When they get careless about reading God's Word, they may think of Jimmy, who works so hard for so little gain. I wonder how many lives haven't been touched by Jimmy's ministry. Don't you wish that more people had something of Jimmy's trait of faithfulness? I wish that some of you were more like Jimmy. Don't you wish that more people had the deep desire that Jimmy has to read and study God's Word? I wish more of you had his desire.

IMAGERY

Our culture tends to belittle imagery: "It's just your imagination." Imagery is looked on as pictures in a story book: nice, but not necessary. This attitude assumes that imagery belongs to children, to the world of the fantastic instead of the world of the real. It is the imagery of a message, however, that helps stimulate the listener. It may be necessary for the preacher to think as a child, and see imaginatively, to present God's truth in a moving manner. Those who listen also have a child inside who delights in an imaginative presentation. Cultural dogmas aside, images move as well as persuade people and so accomplish a major purpose in preaching.

Imagery supports emotional language especially when coupled with repetition, when images pile up, forming layer upon layer.[2] The higher the heaping of the images, the greater the impact. Jude conveys excitement when he writes of corrupted Christianity.

> Woe to them! For they have taken the way of Cain; they have rushed for profit into Balaam's error; they have been destroyed in Korah's rebellion. These men are blemishes at your love feasts, eating with you without the slightest qualm—shepherds who feed only themselves. They are clouds without rain, blown along by the wind; autumn trees, without fruit and uprooted—twice dead. They are wild waves of the sea, foaming up

their shame; wandering stars, for whom the blackest
darkness has been reserved forever (Jude 11–13).

Jude breaks the rules. He mixes metaphors with an egg
beater. Yet his careless language is effective. Look how he
piles image upon image. Who would want to identify with
the group he attacks after hearing all that?

ANTITHESIS

Antithesis is a rhetorical device that catches the attention of the listener. The orator's bag contains many such
devices. But be warned. These devices quickly turn to vices.
Let them be natural and unaffected. Too much attention to
the niceties of style results in a deterioration of speech. If
wisely and purposefully used, however, they assist the
content by catching the attention of the listener. The contrast
of words or ideas in an antithetical sentence elicits involve-
ment. Contrast following contrast deepens the impact.

Therefore this is what the Sovereign LORD says:

"My servants will eat,
but you will go hungry;
my servants will drink,
but you will go thirsty;
my servants will rejoice,
but you will be put to shame.
My servants will sing
out of the joy of their hearts,
but you will cry out
from anguish of heart" (Isa. 65:13–14).

Don't be so callous; rather, show compassion. Instead of
hardness, put on kindness. Kill off pride; wake up humility.
Don't let bitterness take root; let forgiveness blossom. Put an
end to this war; may peace rule. Put aside your dissension;
work for unity.

When the preacher places contrast on top of contrast, the
effect is heightened and the impact of what he says will be
greater.

PERSONIFICATION

"O Jerusalem, Jerusalem, you who kill the prophets and stone those sent to you, how often I have longed to gather your children together, as a hen gathers her chicks under her wings, but you were not willing" (Matt. 23:37).

> Sing for joy, O heavens, for the LORD has done
>   this;
>   shout aloud, O earth beneath.
> Burst into song, you mountains,
>   you forests and all your trees (Isa. 44:23).

"A voice is heard in Ramah,
  mourning and great weeping,
Rachel weeping for her children
  and refusing to be comforted,
  because her children are no more" (Jer. 31:15).

Where, O death, is your victory? (1 Cor. 15:55).

When intelligence, language, or other human attributes are given to inanimate objects or ideas, it pulls the thought down into the world of experience and appeals to daily incidents in the lives of people. Sometimes it makes the absent or even the dead come forth to speak.

> O Paul can you answer our question? Can you solve our problem?

It may give voice to the inanimate world.

> Listen to the mountains sing. What message do you hear? "Our God is majesty, and power, and glory." What a song they sing to his praise!

The possibilities are endless. Personification adds an often-needed note of drama to any message.

REPETITION

The important tool of repetition lays block upon block and line upon line until the force of the message strikes home. If ill used, it adds to dullness. Who likes to hear something said all over again? The kind of repetition that stirs the listener impresses the thought upon him. The preacher not only announces the thought, but comes back to it again, and then another time. He may vary the repetition by approaching the thought from different sides, by piling new ideas onto the repetition, or by applying it a different way. He hasn't succumbed to mere repetition, though that can be effective, but he uses a repetition coupled with variety. When repetition joins hands with other aspects of language, it heightens the emotional impact.

The figure of speech called *climax* makes a clever use of repetition without stifling variety. It repeats a word from the previous sentence and continues that pattern for several clauses or sentences. Joel used it:

> What the locust swarm has left
>   the great locusts have eaten;
> what the great locusts have left
>   the young locusts have eaten;
> what the young locusts have left
>   other locusts have eaten (Joel 1:4).

Consider the impact of the repetitions in Amos 4:6–12. The prophet counts the blessings and judgments of the Lord and then states, "Yet you have not returned to me." He picks up the refrain, not once, not twice, but five times before he concludes with the challenging words, "Prepare to meet your God, O Israel." Each repetition raises the impact of what he says, and the listener cannot remain unmoved.

Augustine, in a sermon on giving, says:

> One of the Psalms teaches us an important truth, and perhaps it is the answer to our question. It says: "O you children of men, how long will you be dull of heart" (Ps. 4:3, 4)? How long did that tree continue—that tree of three years barrenness? O you children of men, how long will you be dull of heart? What does dullness of heart mean? Why do you love vanity, and seek after lying? In response to these queries, it tells us what must

be sought: "Know that the Lord has magnified his Holy One." Christ has now come; He has been magnified; He has risen and has ascended into heaven; His name is now being preached throughout the world. How long will you be dull of heart? Let these past happenings be sufficient. Now that the Holy One has been magnified, how long will you be dull of heart? After three years what is left but the axe? How long will you be dull of heart? Why do you love vanity and seek after lying? Even after Christ has been magnified, are the vain things, the useless things, the pompous and fleeting things still being sought after? Truth is now crying aloud; is vanity still being sought after? How long will you be dull of heart?[3]

How long can people remain dull of heart if the speaker hammers the thought home again and again?

QUESTION CLUSTERS

A single question has some power to prompt a response. When the questions tumble one after another, the effect is multiplied. A grouping of questions tugs several times on the shirt-sleeve of the listener. Listen to a preacher known for his questions:

The blood of the lamb on the lintel and the door-posts of the houses of the Israelites in Egypt saved them and spared them; and the one sign that is looked for on all who would approach and draw nigh unto God is the mark of the blood of the Son of God. Is it on you? If it is, you have a free right of entry . . . into the "holiest of all," into the very presence of God Himself. Are you there, have you been there? Do you pray with confidence and assurance? Do you know God? Are you enjoying fellowship with Him?[4]

PROGRESSION

A sermon does more than give facts and ideas. The preacher's task is not like shoveling gravel into a wheelbarrow. He's a shepherd who leads. His thoughts and words direct his people.

The best kind of architecture shows movement. The artist leads the eye. So let the sermon lead the mind and heart. Make it move. Let it build. Take people by the hand into the valleys and up the mountains. Language plays a vital role in leading the minds of the people.

Little words often point the way. When the preacher says "if," "when," "since," or "because," you know he leads you down some kind of path and you will soon arrive at a conclusion. When the sermon uses a string of "if's" or similar road markers, tension begins to build until it cries for release. Progression and question clusters can be combined to focus the thinking of the listener.

> When Jesus set his face to Jerusalem, what was his goal? When he left Bethany, where was he going? When he descended the hill on a donkey, where would he dismount? When he gathered with the disciples in the upper room, what was his plan? When he prayed Gethsemane's prayer and looked into that awful cup, what did he see? When Jesus was betrayed, where did they take him? When he was sentenced, where did they send him? When he dragged his cross outside the city, where was he going? What was his destination? What was the name of that hill? Do you know that place? Have you been there? at the cross? where the great Redeemer died?

THE SECOND PERSON

When you speak to people as God's representative, speak to them as the representative of God. Don't always tell them *about* the message found in the Bible. Proclaim to them the Word of God. If you do, you will use that important little pronoun "you."[5]

Some people like dialogue. The best kind of dialogue occurs when God speaks to people and the people answer with faith and obedience. That's hard to accomplish when the sermon conveys ideas far removed from the personal in a manner that leaves people flat.

> This is what the Word of God says to God's people on this occasion.

A direct expression says,

> Listen! The Lord is speaking to you this moment.

That conveys the truth that this is an exciting hour, a time when the Lord is addressing his people.

George Whitefield's evangelistic style didn't shrink from a direct approach to people.

> Perhaps some of you here are saying, "burning bush, a bush burnt and not consumed. I do not know what to make of this nonsense." Come, come, go on, I am used to it, and I guess what are the thoughts of your heart. I pray God that every one of you here may be afraid of your heart. I pray God that every one of you here may be afraid of comfort, lest they should be tossed about by the devil. What is it I have said? How have I talked in such an unintelligible manner? Why, say you, what do you mean by a burning bush? Why, thou art the very man. How so? Why, you are burning with the devil in your hearts; you are burning with foppery, with nonsense, with the lust of the flesh . . . ; and if you do not get out of this state, as Lot said to his sons-in-law, ere long you shall be burning in hell and not consumed: the same angel of the covenant who spake to Moses out of the bush, he shall ere long descend, surrounded with millions of the heavenly host, and sentence you to everlasting burnings. O you frighten me! Did you think I did not intend to frighten you? Would to God I might frighten you enough! I believe it will be no harm for you to be frightened out of hell, to be frightened out of an unconverted state. God pluck you as brands out of that burning.[6]

You may disagree with the way Whitefield applied the passage, but you can't argue with his direct style. Count the times he made use of the second person. Whitefield succeeded in moving people in part by his use of that little word "you." You can learn from him.

HYPERBOLE

The word *hyperbole* comes from two Greek words: *huper*, meaning "above, beyond"; and *ballo*, "to throw or cast." Hyperbole throws above or stretches and exaggerates reality.

If hyperbole stretches and exaggerates, you may assume it has nothing to do with truth, especially God's truth. Preachers, of all people, shouldn't exaggerate. Hyperbole must be a fancy word for "hype."

The Bible, however, puts hyperbole to good use. John concludes his gospel with a beautiful hyperbole. "I suppose that even the whole world would not have room for the books that would be written" (John 21:25). Acts 17:21 says, "All . . . spent their time doing nothing but talking about and listening to the latest ideas."

Take a closer look at these two passages. The world is a large place. Do you really think that it would take all that room to tell of everything that Jesus did? And did Luke want to say that every human being in Athens did nothing other than speak of or listen to new ideas? Didn't they work or sleep or eat? Didn't Athenians ever discuss something old? Why did he state it this way? He wants the reader to sit up and take notice. It's like **BOLD-PRINT LETTERS** on a written page. It commands you to take note.

Jesus used this figure of speech for radical purposes. "If your right eye causes you to sin, gouge it out and throw it away. It is better for you to lose one part of your body than for your whole body to be thrown into hell. And if your right hand causes you to sin . . ." (Matt. 5:29–30). Jesus teaches the need to put sin away. Does he really want us to respond by mutilating ourselves? How many one-eyed or one-handed Christians have you met? Jesus employs the shock technique found in hyperbole to move people to respond.

He does so several times. Think of the mustard seed, moving mountains, and the camel and the needle. "How can you say to your brother, 'Let me take the speck out of your eye,' when all the time there is a plank in your own eye?" (Matt. 7:4). Something of irony lurks in that statement. When the Lord couples caricature with hyperbole, then the effect is most telling.

Jesus employed this shock technique with "religious" people who endured the teaching of the scribes. It was designed to "get through" to people who were awash with all kinds of half-truths and false teaching. He didn't come with another variety of religion. He did more than tickle ears with interesting ideas. He proclaimed a radical kingdom message. His claim is exclusive. There is no life apart from him. He laid claim to people's faith and allegiance. Hyperbole, as Jesus used it, reflects that urgency.

The preacher also brings the kingdom message. It calls for faith and allegiance from people today. So the ambassador of Jesus Christ does not fear shock treatment and dares to counter dull resistance with caricature. Consider this:

> There's a disease about. Some have already died of it. It has a name. It's called tubal amblyopia. Tubal amblyopia is a condition that afflicts a good many people and a lot of Christians, too. Tubal amblyopia is as common as the cold. What is it? you ask. Have I been exposed? Let me explain.
>
> The word *amblyopia* means dim-sightedness. Many Christians cannot see well. Dim vision clouds their view of God's Word and God's world. They see only a dim outline of the bright and glorious reality. What's the cause of this dim-sightedness? That's explained by the word *tubal*. "Tubal" comes from "tube." Many people, countless Christians among them, see their world through a tube. That's about the only view they get. They wouldn't know that there are stars in the sky unless they saw it on the tube.
>
> There are symptoms of this sometimes fatal disease. When tubal personalities loom larger than biblical ones, when Johnny looms larger than John, then the disease is surely in an advanced state. When you find yourself commenting about tubal advertisements—commercials

I think they're called—then the condition is certainly terminal.

What's the cure? Radical surgery. A wire cutter is a necessity. Perform surgery on that brown wire that leads from the wall. Don't pull the plug. The disease so grips a person that you will plug it right back in at the first twitch of an eyeball. After cutting the umbilical cord to the tube, lift it up, carry it out of doors, drop it into the trash can. Be sure to do this on pickup day, or the disease will compel you to rescue and restore the beloved tube.

That's just the beginning of the cure. Spend two hours a day looking at and talking to your wife. This disease does strange things to marriages. Be sure it's your wife. You may have forgotten what the woman in your life looks like. Next, turn to your children. Take a good look. My, haven't they grown? Turn on to God's great outdoors as well. Then dust off the Book—the one you haven't read in an intelligent and heartfelt way in years. Open its pages and learn to see again in the most wonderful, clear-eyed way possible. By the grace of God, by careful attention to this cure, and with a lot of help from family and friends, you just might escape further ravages of this deadly disease.

Conclusion

If you have persisted to this point, you do have an interest in better preaching. Where, you may wonder, does the path lead now? Have we come to the end of the journey, or is it the beginning? That depends on you. If you reflect on the principles found in this little book, among others, and put into practice some of the suggestions, then for you the path to better preaching may continue.

I urge the preacher who reads this to join those who seek to lift preaching to greater heights. Some have written an obituary for preaching. Contrary to these opinions, preaching survives its announced demise. Although the church of today demands a variety of skills, none is as important as preaching. There's a renewed interest in this task today. If the trend continues, I suspect that you will see the estimate of preaching improve until it takes its rightful place as the minister's glorious task. I hope you can find in this book something to help you make your way toward the goal of better preaching.

Acknowledgments

This book is part of a Doctor of Ministry project at Westminster Theological Seminary in California. I thank members of the faculty of that institution for the encouragement they have given. The Director of Advanced Studies, Dr. Jay E. Adams, must be singled out for many helpful suggestions.

I thank my congregation in Crown Point for the opportunity to study.

A thank-you to the following pastors for putting these materials to the test in their preaching: Donald Den Hartog, Donald Draayer, Gilbert Kamps, Howard Matson, Ted Medema, Donald Munson, and Peter Vosteen.

I also want to thank my partner in life, to whom this book is dedicated, for the hours of reading, the many suggestions, and the encouragement given.

William H. Kooienga

Notes

Chapter 1

1. Aristotle, *Rhetoric* III.12.2.

2. Quintilian, *Institutes* VIII.13–24.

3. Aristotle, *Rhetoric* III.2.2.

Chapter 2

1. Gerhard Delling, *"Huperecho, huperoche,"* in *Theological Dictionary of the New Testament,* ed. Gerhard Friedrich and Gerhard Kittel, 10 vols. (Grand Rapids: Eerdmans, 1964–1976), 8:523–24.

2. Luke employs the *enthymeme* (rhetorical syllogism) in Acts 2:25–36 to summarize Peter's preaching. Major premise: Resurrection without corruption was foretold by David. Minor premise: God raised up Jesus (and we are witnesses). Conclusion: God has made Jesus both Lord and Christ. Paul uses a similar kind of argument in Acts 17:3. The Messiah must suffer and rise from the dead. The only one who fits this description is Christ. The conclusion: "This Jesus I am proclaiming to you is the Christ" (v. 3).

3. Note words like *tekmerion* (Acts 1:3). The word comes from the Greek and is not used in the Septuagint to translate any Hebrew concept. Aristotle (*Rhetoric* 1.2.16) defines it as "a compelling sign." Acts 17:1–4 says that Paul argued (*dielexetō*) and persuaded (*peithetō*). See also Acts 19:8, 26; 28:23; and 2 Corinthians 5:11. "The typical Greek concepts of persuading and convincing are notably absent from the Hebrew tongue" (Rudolf Bultmann, *"Peithō,"* *Theological Dictionary of the New Testament,* 6:1).

4. Quintilian, *Institutes* VIII.11.

5. Hans Dieter Betz cites evidence of rhetoric in Scripture. "Paul's letter to the Galatians is an example of the 'apologetic letter' genre" (Betz, *Galatians* [Philadelphia: Fortress Press, 1979], 14). "The apologetic letter . . . presupposes the real or fictitious situation of the court of law . . . " (ibid., 24). Nevertheless, Augustine says, "For it is because they are eloquent that they exemplify these rules; it is not that they use them in order to be eloquent" (Aurelius Augustine, *On Christian Doctrine,* in *The Works of Aurelius Augustine,* ed. Marcus Dods [Edinburgh: T. and T. Clark, 1873], 123).

Chapter 3

1. Aurelius Augustine, *On Christian Doctrine,* in *The Works of Aurelius Augustine,* ed. Marcus Dods [Edinburgh: T. and T. Clark, 1873], 121.

2. Ibid., 144.

3. Ibid., 124.

4. Ibid., 153.

5. Quoted in Erich Auerbach, *Literary Language and Its Public* (London: Routledge and Kegan Paul, 1965), 35.

6. Augustine, *On Christian Doctrine,* 146.

7. Ibid., 148–49.

8. Auerbach, *Literary Language and Its Public,* 56.

Chapter 4

1. For an expanded discussion of this form see James Murphy, *Medieval Eloquence* (Berkeley: University of California Press, 1978), 114ff.

Chapter 5

1. Martin Luther, *Easter Book,* trans. Roland Bainton (Philadelphia: Fortress, 1983), 29–30.

Notes

2. "The Eleventh Sermon," in *John Calvin's Sermons on Ephesians,* (Edinburgh: Banner of Truth Trust, 1973), 165.

3. Walter J. Ong, "Peter Ramus and the Naming of Methodism," *Journal of the History of Ideas* 14 (April 1953): 243.

4. H. Richard Niebuhr and Daniel D. Williams, *The Ministry in Historical Perspective,* 2d ed. (San Francisco: Harper & Row, 1983), 188.

5. Phyllis Jones and Nicholas Jones, eds., *Salvation in New England* (Austin: University of Texas Press, 1977), 104–116.

6. Niebuhr and Williams, *The Ministry in Historical Perspective,* 188.

7. Ong, "Peter Ramus and the Naming of Methodism."

Chapter 6

1. Harry Fosdick, "Faith and Immortality," in *What Is Vital in Religion* (New York: Harper Bros., 1955), 237.

2. Edward Steimle, *God the Stranger* (Philadelphia: Fortress, 1979), 7.

3. John Crossan, *The Dark Interval* (Niles, Ill.: Argus Communications, 1975), 43–44.

4. Ibid., 44.

Chapter 7

1. The three purposes are widely recognized and sometimes unintentionally described. "We ought not to begin with severe reproof but with doctrine, that men may be gently drawn by it. When plain and simple doctrine is not sufficient, proofs must be added. But if even this method produces no good effect, it then becomes necessary to employ greater vehemence" (John Calvin, *Commentary on Isaiah,* vol. 1 [Grand Rapids: Eerdmans, 1958], 242).

Chapter 8

1. Aristotle, *Rhetoric* III.2.2.

2. C. S. Lewis, *Studies in Words* (Cambridge: Cambridge University Press, 1960), 223.

3. With apologies to Gelett Burgess, who wrote a chapter on the short word with the one-syllable kind in Marvin S. Zuckerman, ed., *Words, Words, Words* (London: Glencoe Press, 1980), 172ff.

4. William Morris and Mary Morris, *Morris Dictionary of Word and Phrase Origins* (New York: Harper & Row, 1977).

5. Zuckerman, *Words, Words, Words*, 273.

Chapter 9

1. Rudolf Flesch, *The Art of Plain Talk* (New York: Harper Brothers, 1946), 48.

2. See pages 85–88 for more on imagery.

3. "Wagons," a sermon on Genesis 45:26–28 by the Rev. Esler L. Shuart, preached in the Faith Community Christian Reformed Church of Wyckoff, New Jersey.

4. John Chrysostom, *In Praise of St. Paul* (Boston: St. Paul Editions, 1963), 60.

Chapter 10

1. *Oxford English Dictionary.*

2. Alexander Maclaren, *Leaves From the Tree of Life* (New York: Funk and Wagnalls, n.d.), 87.

3. Steven J. Brown, *Image and Truth: Studies in the Imagery of the Bible* (Rome: Catholic Book Agency, 1955), 11.

4. Charles H. Spurgeon, *The Metropolitan Tabernacle Pulpit* (London: Passmore and Alabaster, 1897), 4.

5. See pages 75–76.

6. Jay E. Adams, *Studies in Preaching*, vol. 1, *Sense Appeal in the Sermons of Charles Haddon Spurgeon* (Nutley, N.J.: Presbyterian and Reformed, 1976).

7. Quintilian, *Institutes* IX.3.100.

8. *The Concordia Pulpit for 1981* (St. Louis: Concordia, 1980), 282.

Chapter 11

1. Roland H. Bainton, trans., *The Martin Luther Christmas Book* (Philadelphia: Westminster, 1958), 71.

2. Eugene Field, as quoted in Robert Claiborne, *Our Marvelous Native Tongue* (New York: Times Books, 1983), 70.

3. Ibid., 72.

4. Jay E. Adams, *Preaching With Purpose* (Phillipsburg, N.J.: Presbyterian and Reformed, 1982), 42ff.

5. Rudolf Flesch, *The Art of Plain Talk* (New York: Harper Brothers, 1946), 69.

6. Ibid., 39.

Chapter 12

1. See also pages 81–83.

2. See also pages 75–76 and 85–88.

3. Aurelius Augustine, "On Almsgiving" *Commentary on the Lord's Sermon on the Mount*, in *The Fathers of the Church*, vol. 2 (Washington: Catholic University of America Press, 1955), 291–92.

4. D. Martin Lloyd-Jones, *God's Way of Reconciliation* (Grand Rapids: Baker, 1972), 185–86.

5. See also pages 91–92.

6. Andrew Blackwood, ed., *The Protestant Pulpit* (Grand Rapids: Baker, 1977), 39.